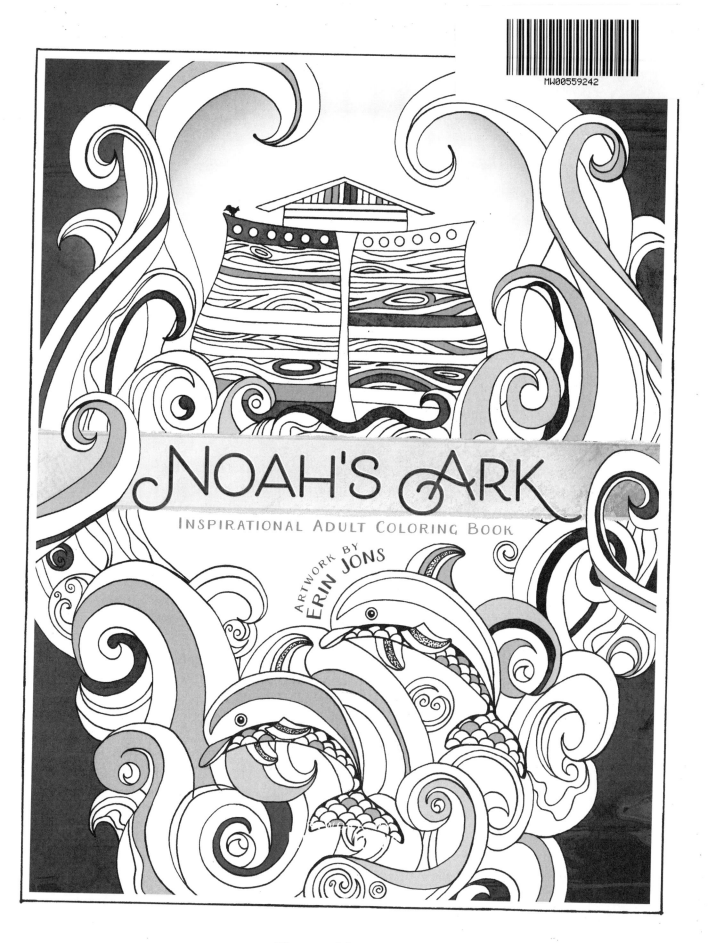

NOAH'S ARK

INSPIRATIONAL ADULT COLORING BOOK

ARTWORK BY
ERIN JONS

BroadStreet
PUBLISHING

BroadStreet Publishing Group LLC
Racine, Wisconsin, USA
Broadstreetpublishing.com

MAJESTIC EXPRESSIONS

Noah's Ark
© 2016 by BroadStreet Publishing

ISBN 978-1-4245-5195-8

Artwork by Erin Jons.

Cover design by Chris Garborg | garborgdesign.com
Compiled and edited by Michelle Winger | literallyprecise.com

Printed in the United States of America.

16 17 18 19 20 21 22   7 6 5 4 3 2 1

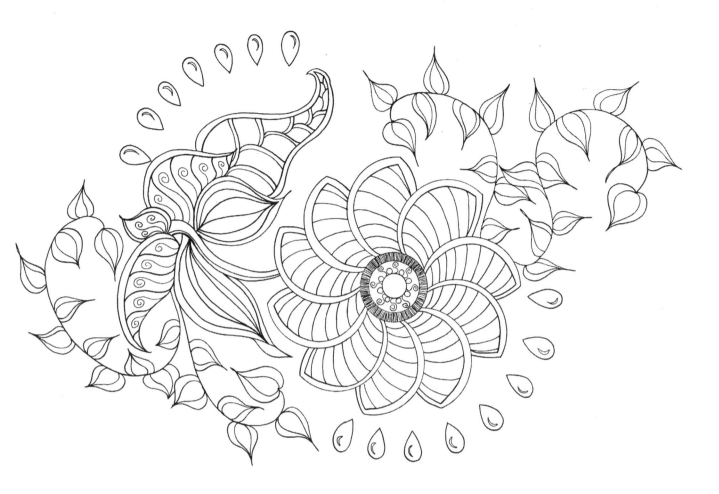

ABOUT THE ILLUSTRATOR

ERIN JONS is a self-taught artist who enjoys the intricacies of creativity. Her relationship with paper and ink began in 1998 as she drew, sketched, and doodled her way through the trials of high school lectures. This relationship has continued in the form of portraits, theatrical set design, and drawing countless coloring pages for her own children. She is humbled and delighted to see her art mingle with God's precious and powerful Word, and prays that time spent with each page will reveal a glimpse of the beauty of Jesus. Erin is happily married with five children in Northern Idaho.

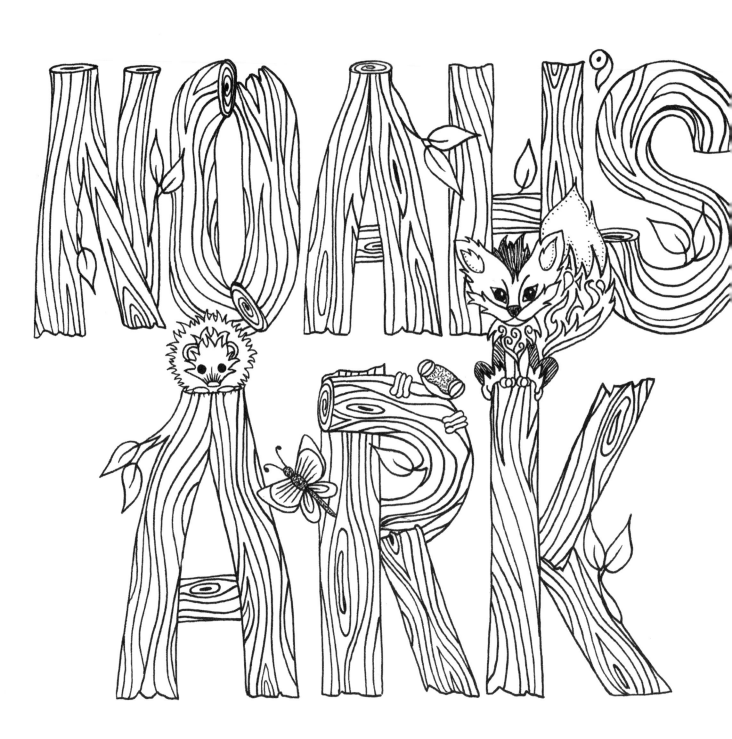

INTRODUCTION

WHY ADULT COLORING BOOKS?

There is plenty of research that shows coloring to be an effective stress reducer. Maybe you picked up this book because you've heard the hype and you're curious. Perhaps you've been looking for a way to relax. Or, if you're like many others we've encountered, you've been looking for a good excuse to color since you "grew up" and coloring books were no longer an acceptable hobby. Over the years, you may have found yourself eager to babysit kids who were fond of coloring, or maybe you have children or grandchildren of your own that need your help filling in the pages of their coloring books.

Finally you hold in your hand your very own adult coloring book. And you have every reason you need to sit down and color. You have entered a stress-free zone. There's no wrong way to color. If you want the grass to be blue and the sky to be green, go right ahead. If you only want to color a portion of a picture, do it. Crayons? Coloring pencils? Markers? It's your choice. This is your book, and this is your time.

Let's take it a step further. While coloring may be a great distraction from all you have going on, the best way to find lasting peace is to spend time with your Creator. As you fill these intricately designed illustrations with the beauty of color, dwell on richness of his Word, the faithfulness of his character, and the depth of his love for you.

"I HAVE TOLD YOU THESE THINGS, SO THAT IN ME YOU MAY HAVE PEACE.
IN THIS WORLD YOU WILL HAVE TROUBLE.
BUT TAKE HEART! I HAVE OVERCOME THE WORLD."
JOHN 16:33 NIV

Happy coloring!

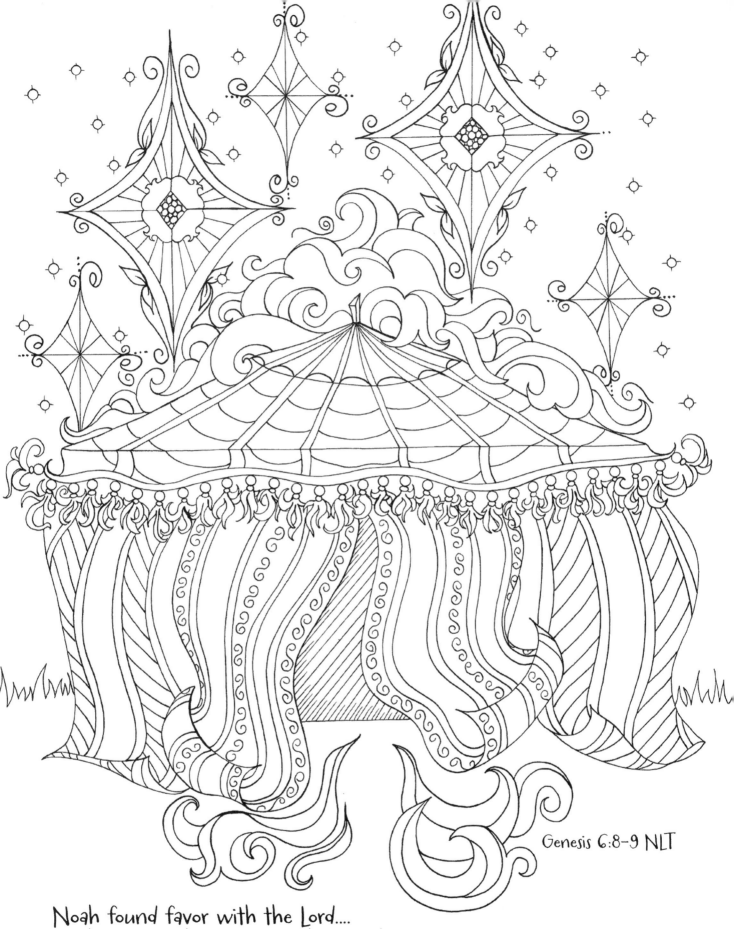

Genesis 6:8-9 NLT

Noah found favor with the Lord....
Noah was a righteous man, the only blameless person
living on earth at the time, and he walked in close fellowship with God.

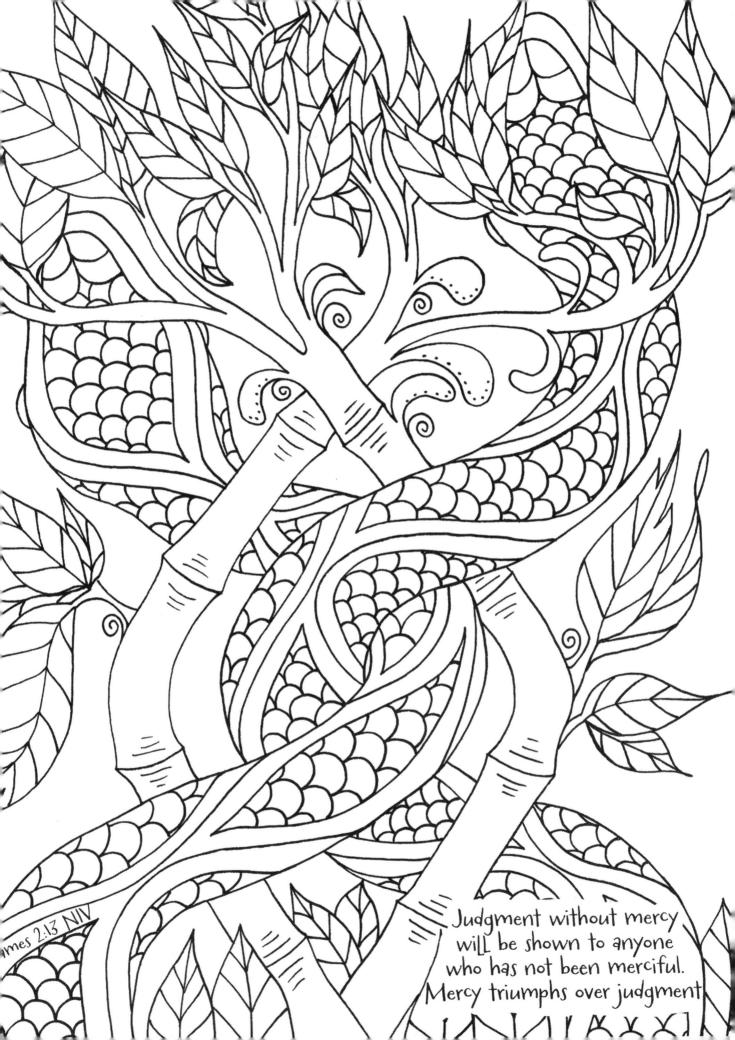

James 2:13 NIV

Judgment without mercy
will be shown to anyone
who has not been merciful.
Mercy triumphs over judgment

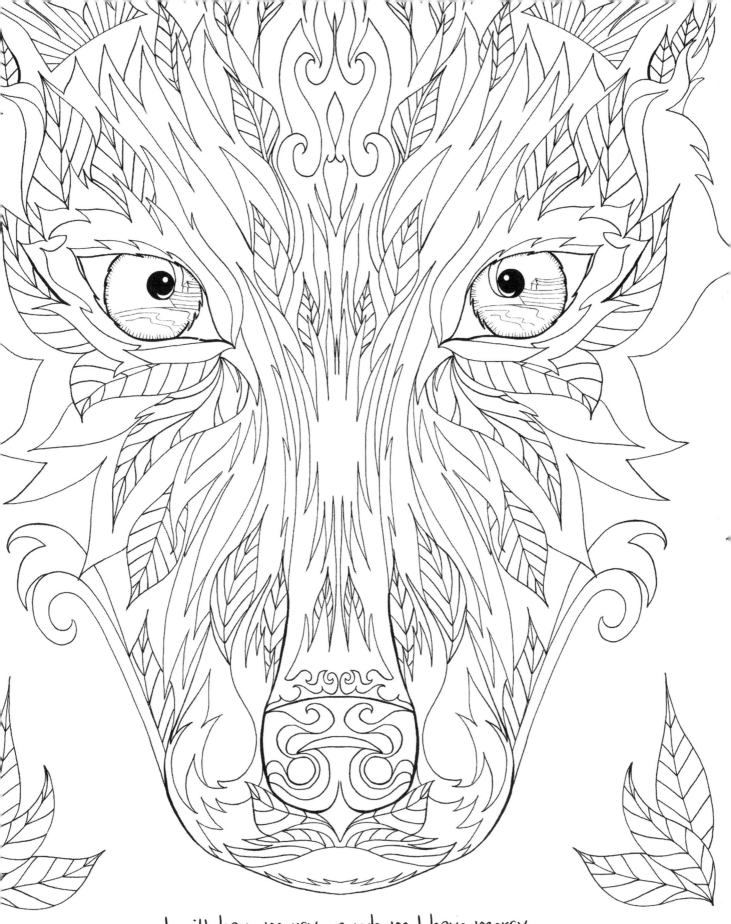

I will have mercy on whom I have mercy,
and I will have compassion on whom I have compassion.
Romans 9:15 ESV

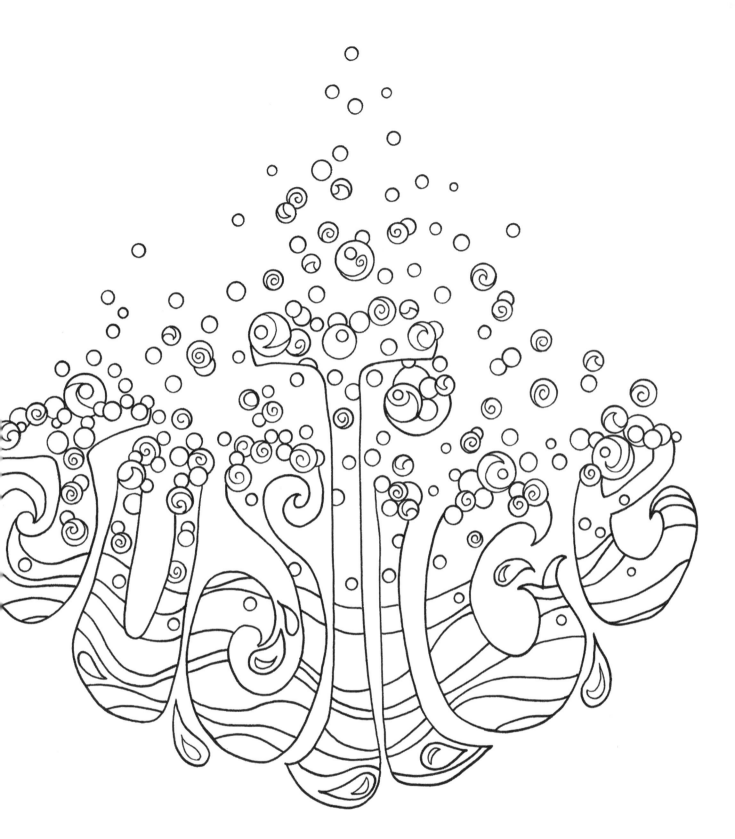

The exercise of justice is joy for the righteous.

Proverbs 21:15 NASB

Build a large boat from cypress wood and waterproof it with tar, inside and out.

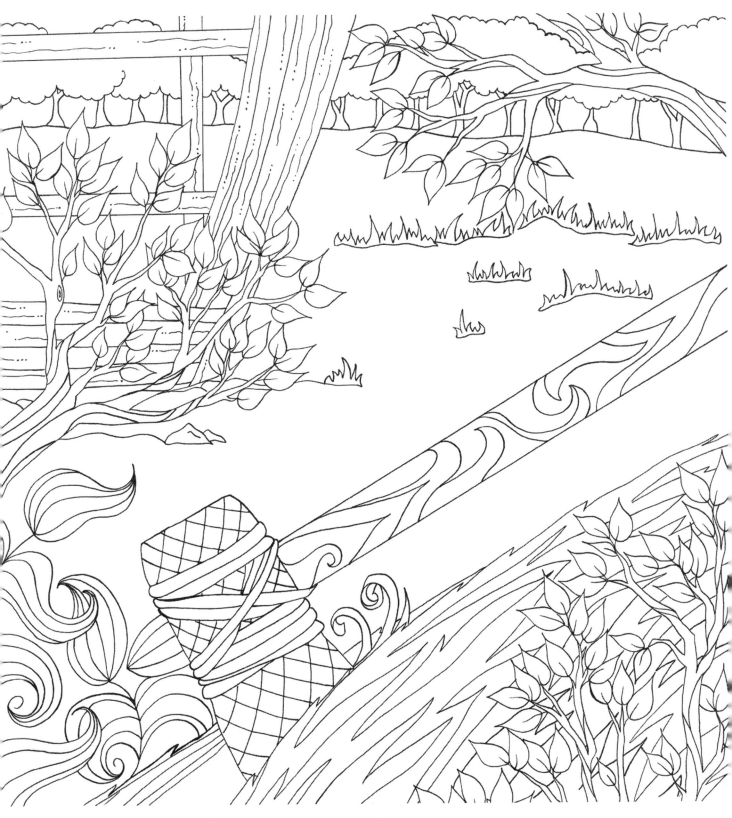

Then construct decks and stalls throughout its interior. Genesis 6:14 NLT

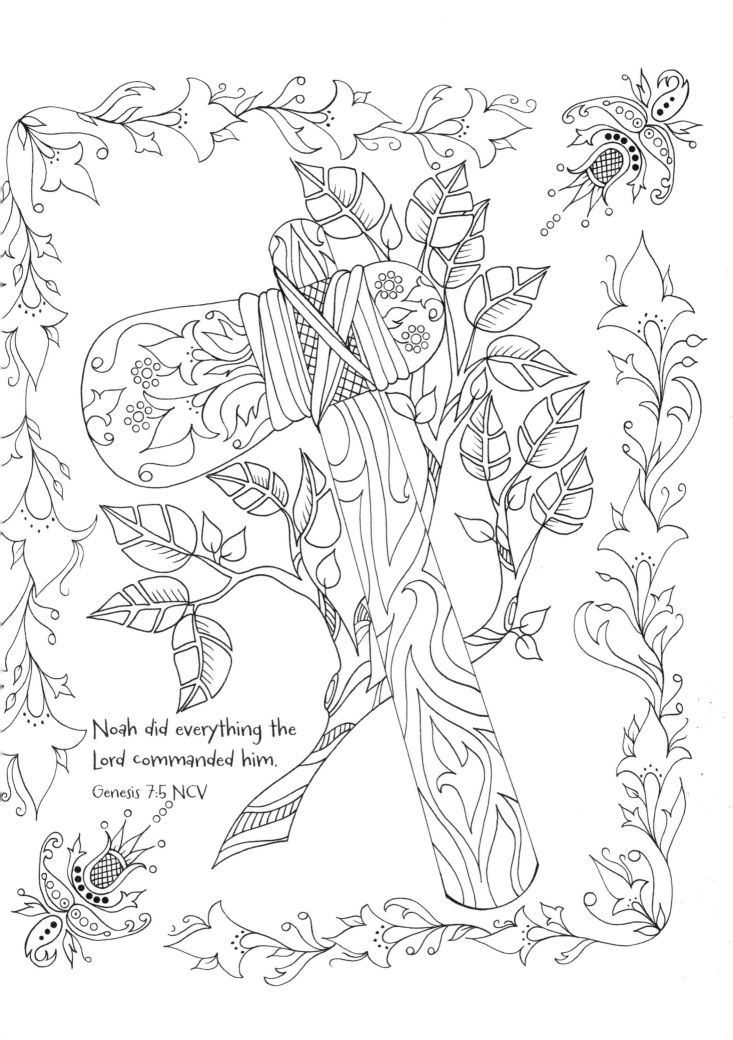

Noah did everything the
Lord commanded him.

Genesis 7:5 NCV

By faith Noah, when warned about things not yet seen,
in holy fear built an ark to save his family.

Hebrews 11:7 NIV

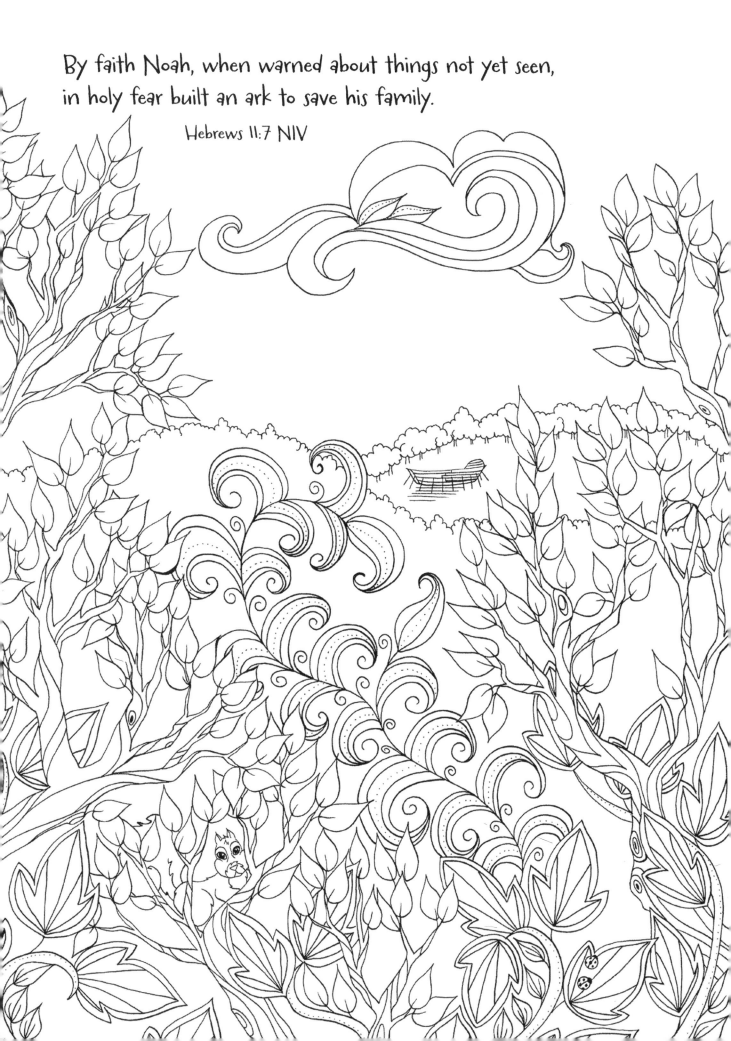

Surely His salvation is near to those who fear Him,
That glory may dwell in our land.

Psalm 85:9 NASB

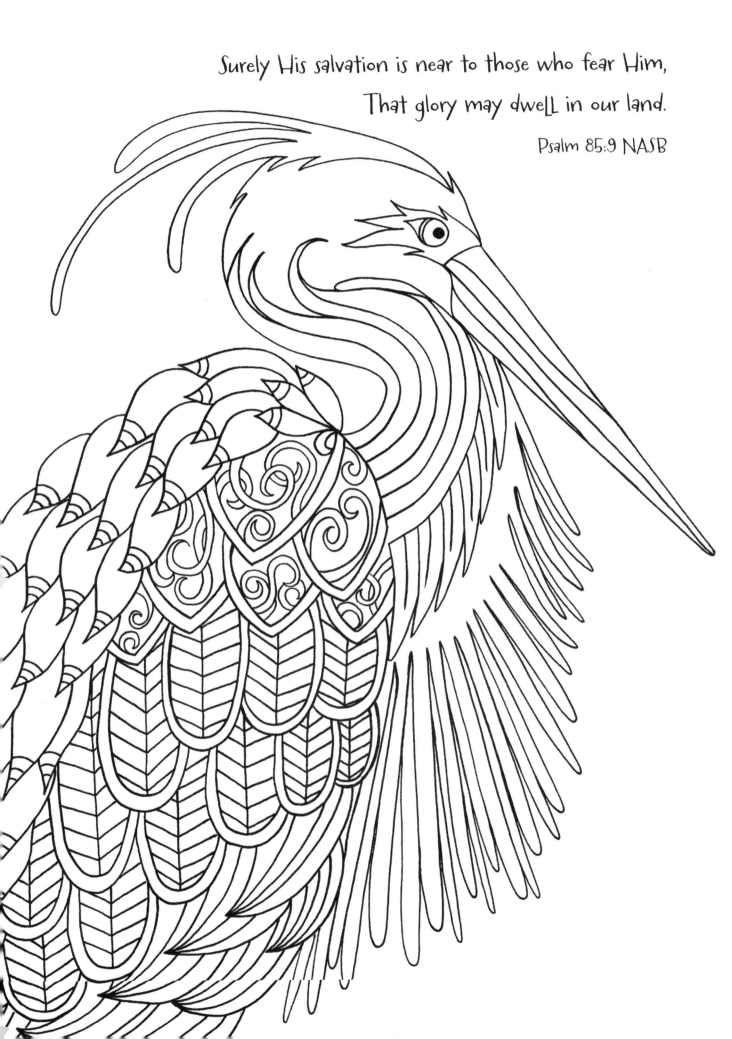

Be sure to take on board enough food for your family
and for all the animals.
Genesis 6:21 NLT

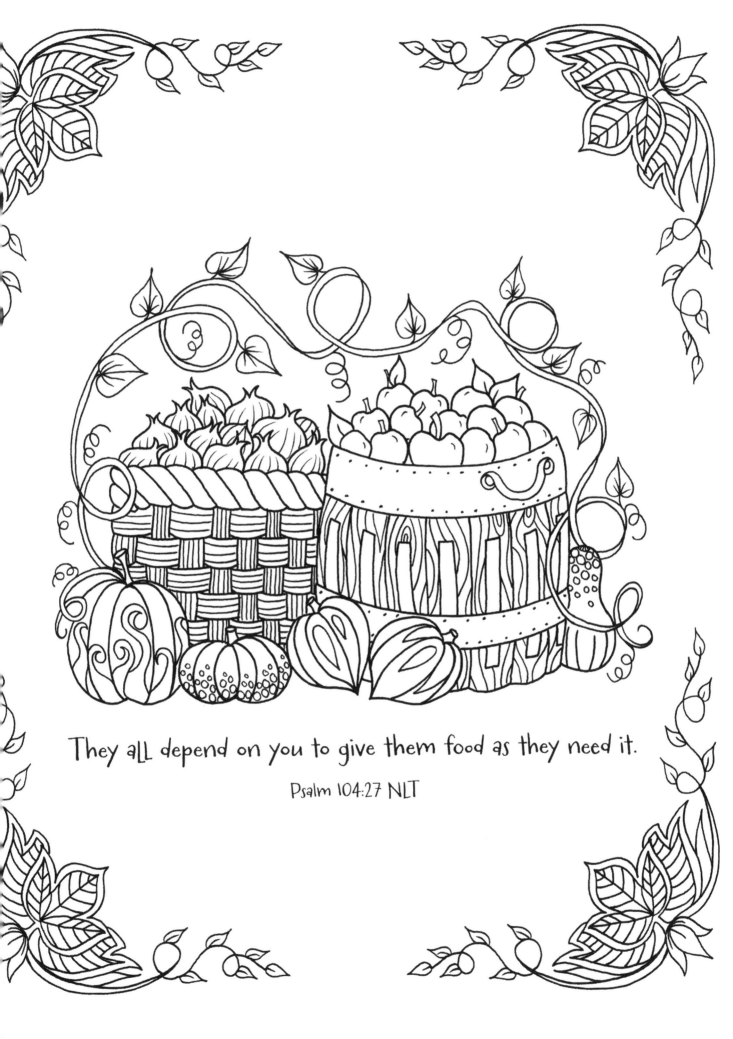

They all depend on you to give them food as they need it.

Psalm 104:27 NLT

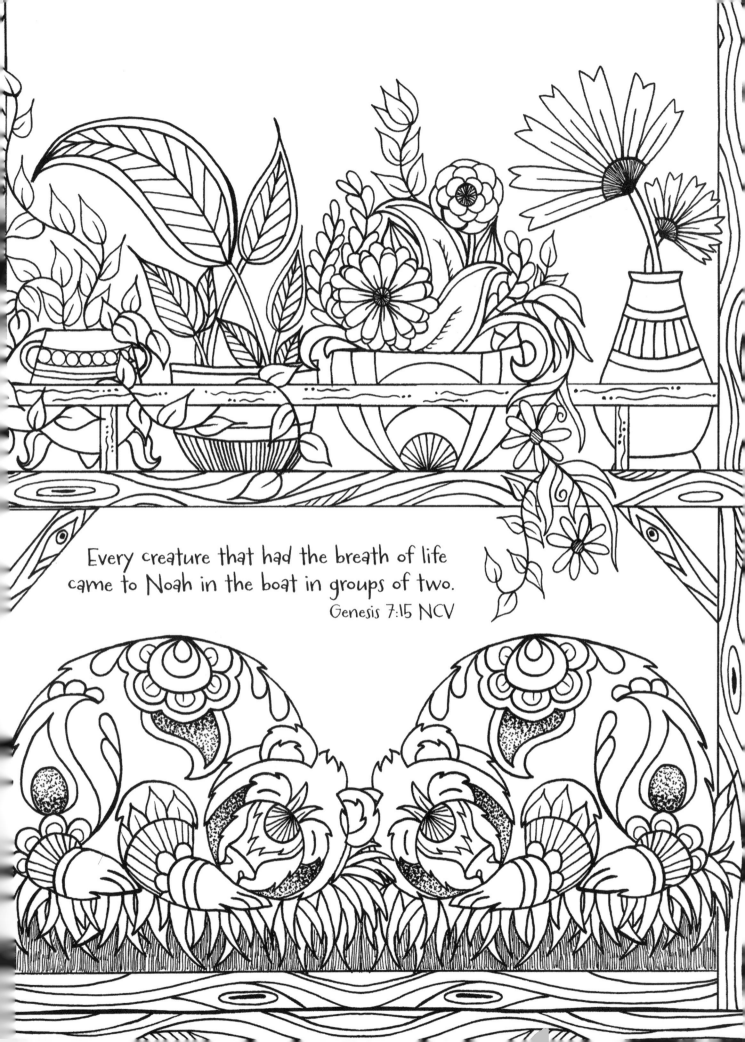

Every creature that had the breath of life came to Noah in the boat in groups of two.

Genesis 7:15 NCV

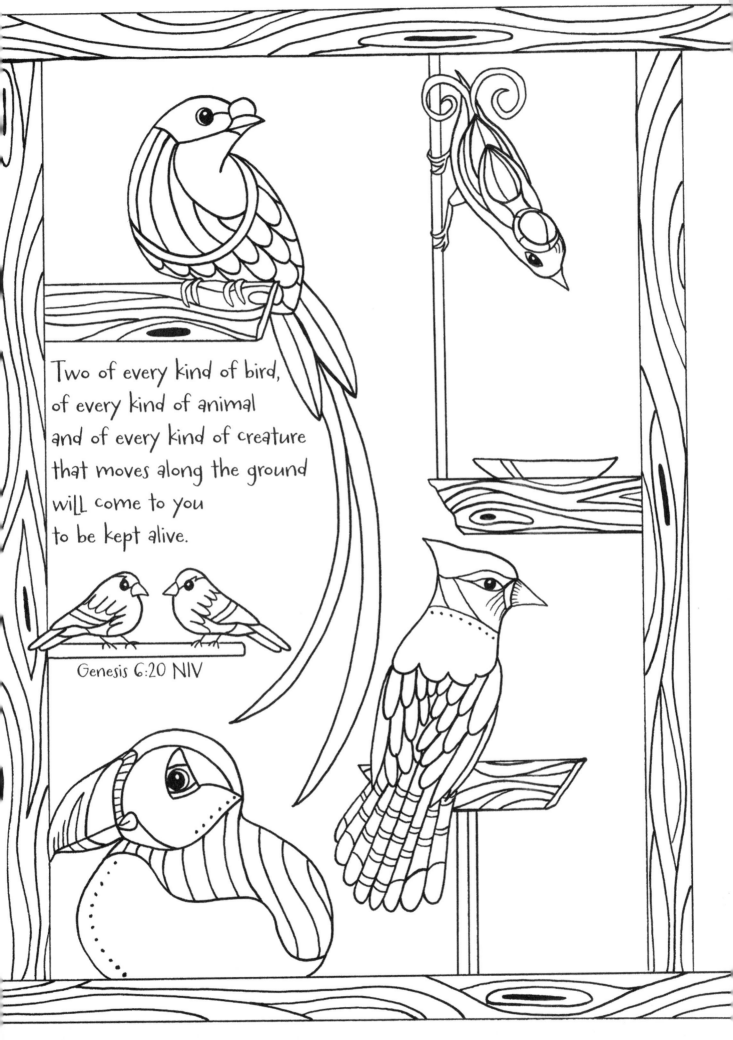

Two of every kind of bird,
of every kind of animal
and of every kind of creature
that moves along the ground
will come to you
to be kept alive.

Genesis 6:20 NIV

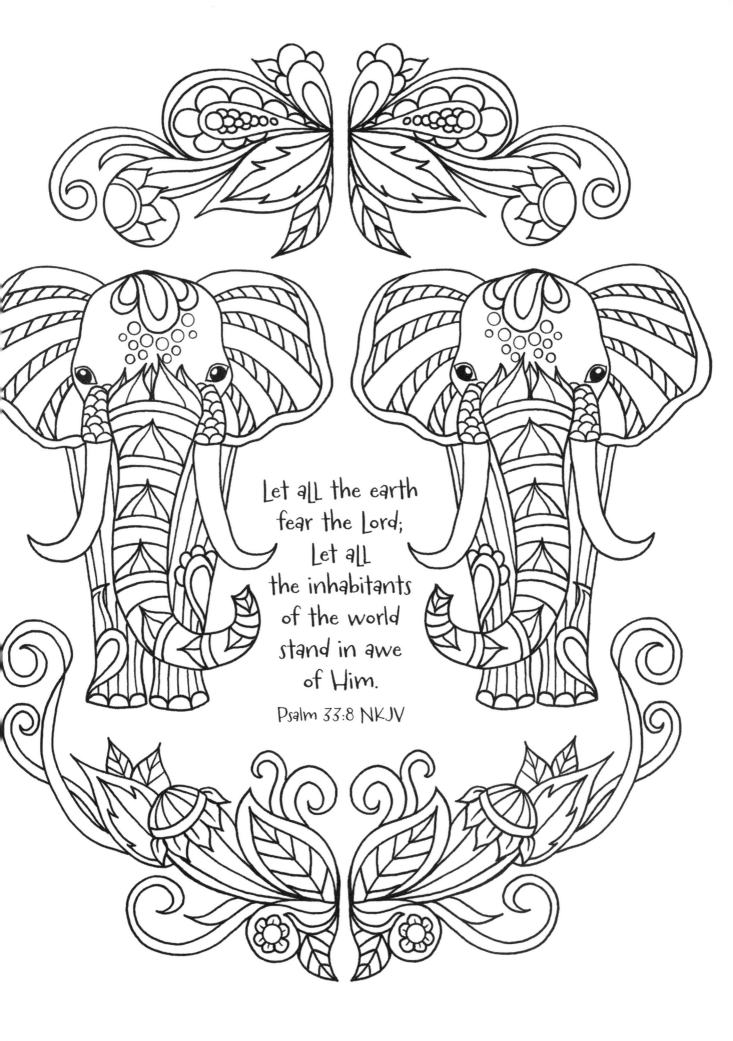

Let all the earth
fear the Lord;
Let all
the inhabitants
of the world
stand in awe
of Him.

Psalm 33:8 NKJV

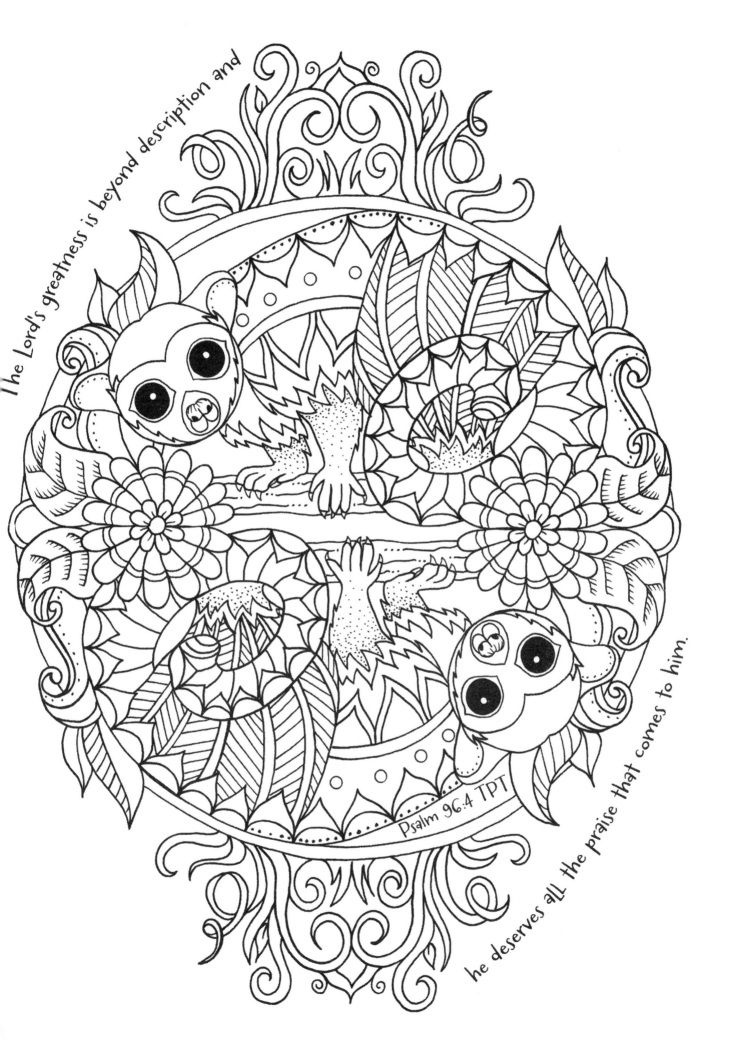

The Lord's greatness is beyond description and

Psalm 96:4 TPT

he deserves all the praise that comes to him.

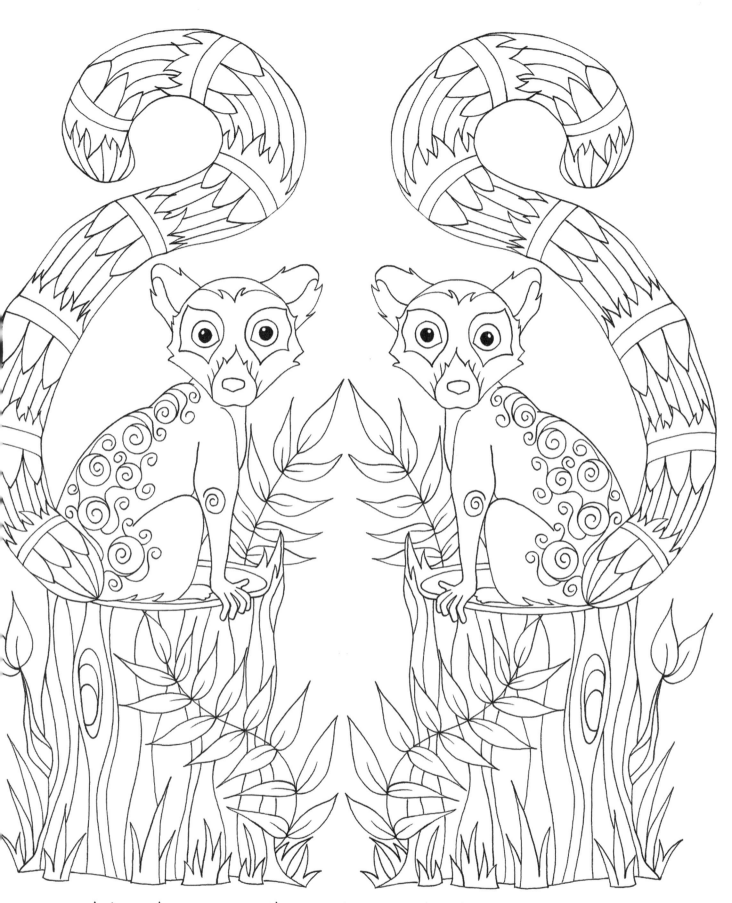

Let us draw near with confidence to the throne of grace,
so that we may receive mercy and find grace to help in time of need.

Hebrews 4:16 NASB

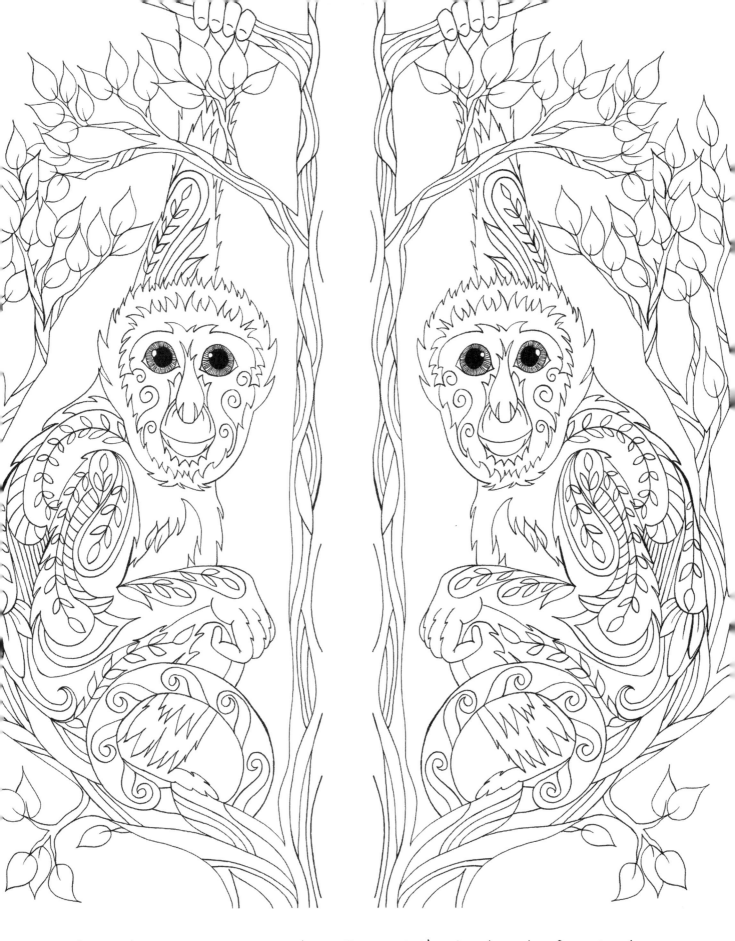

Don't depend on your own wisdom. Respect the Lord and refuse to do wrong.
Proverbs 3:7 NCV

Only serve the Lord and serve Him in truth with all your heart; for consider what great things He has done for you.

1 Samuel 12:24 NASB

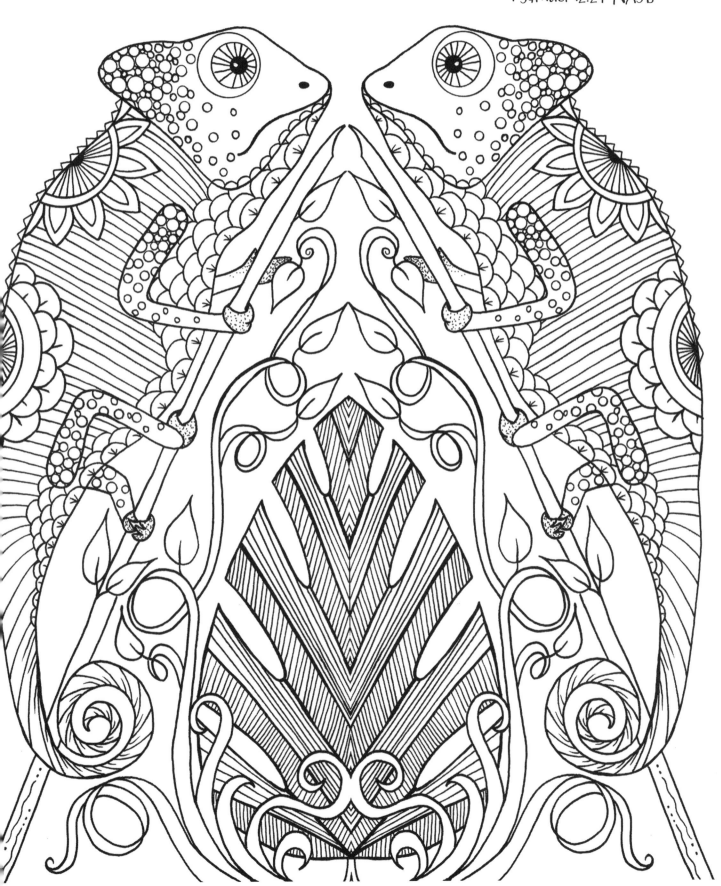

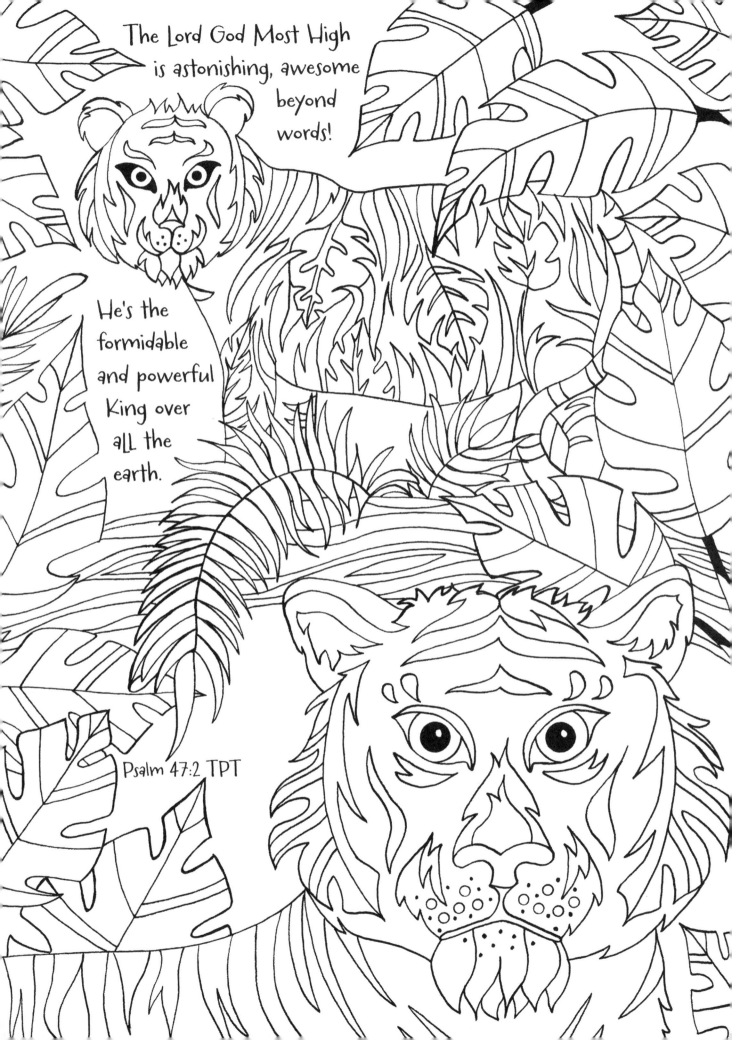

The Lord God Most High
is astonishing, awesome
beyond
words!

He's the
formidable
and powerful
King over
all the
earth.

Psalm 47:2 TPT

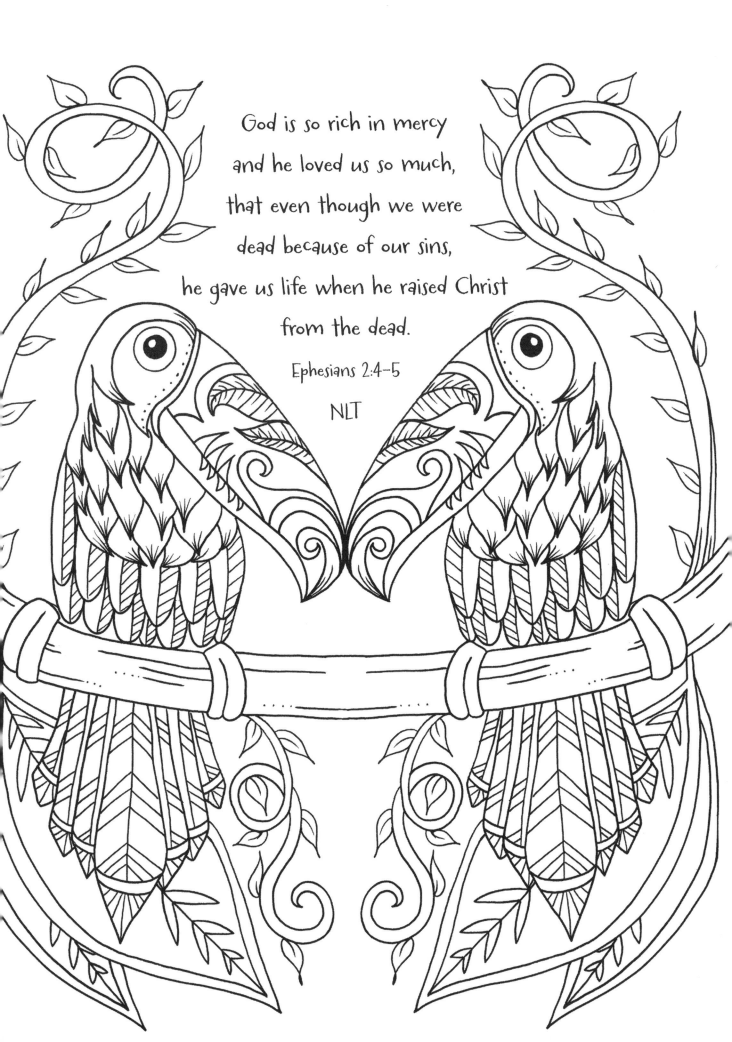

God is so rich in mercy
and he loved us so much,
that even though we were
dead because of our sins,
he gave us life when he raised Christ
from the dead.

Ephesians 2:4–5

NLT

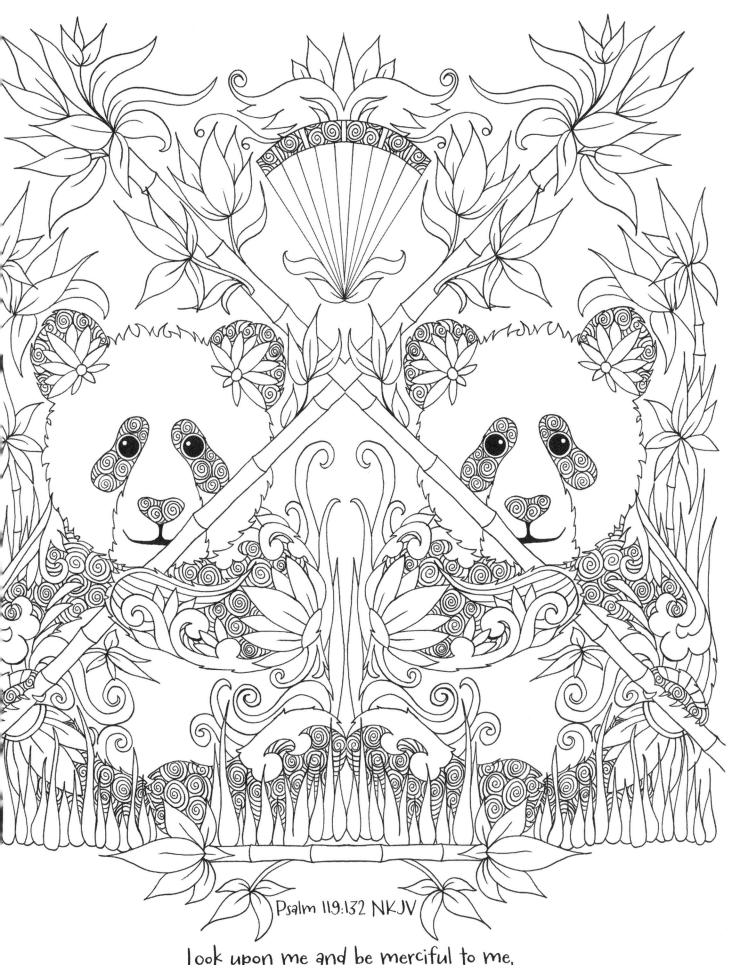

Psalm 119:132 NKJV

Look upon me and be merciful to me,
As Your custom is toward those who love Your name.

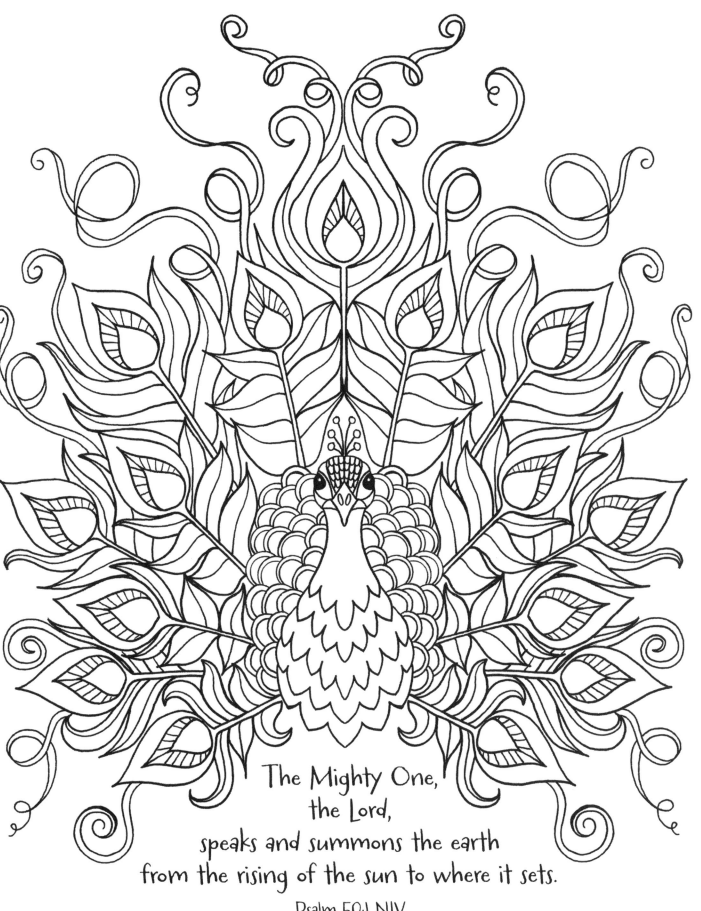

The Mighty One,
the Lord,
speaks and summons the earth
from the rising of the sun to where it sets.

Psalm 50:1 NIV

He is the Rock, his works are perfect, and all his ways are just.

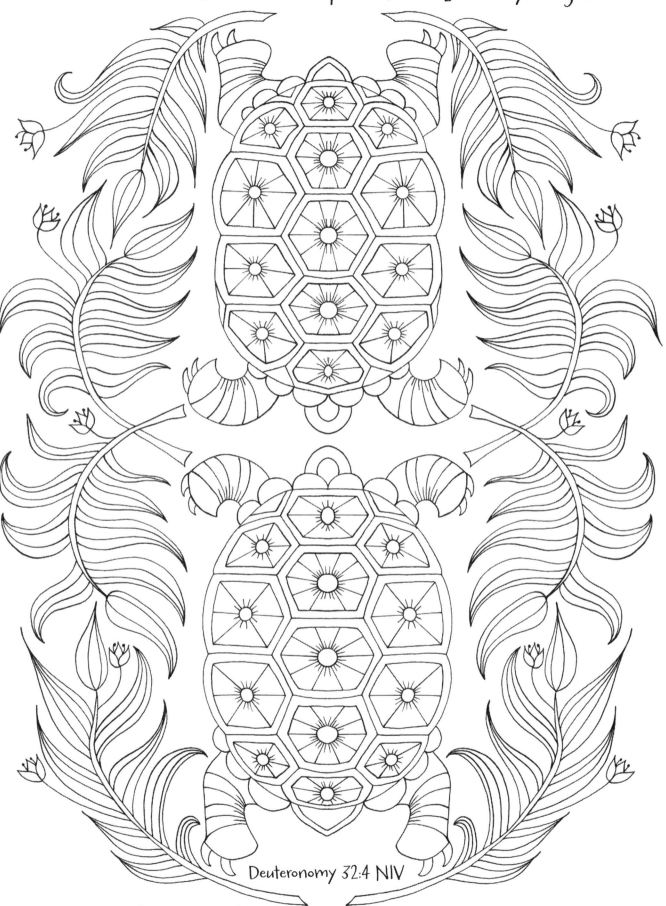

Deuteronomy 32:4 NIV

A faithful God who does no wrong, upright and just is he.

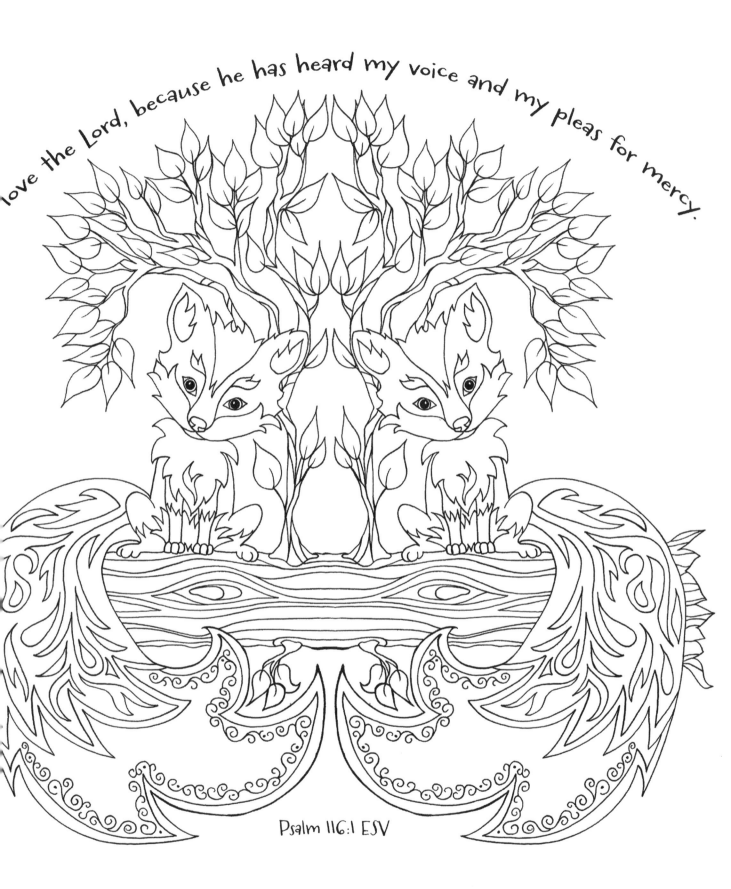

Psalm 116:1 ESV

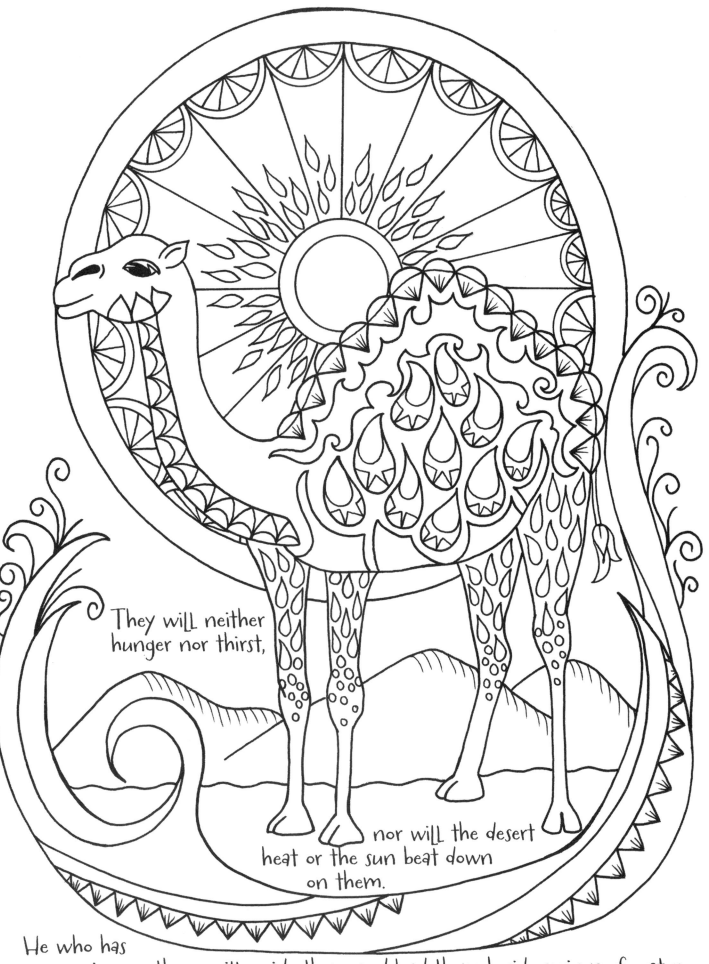

They will neither hunger nor thirst,

nor will the desert heat or the sun beat down on them.

He who has compassion on them will guide them and lead them beside springs of water.

Isaiah 49:10 NIV

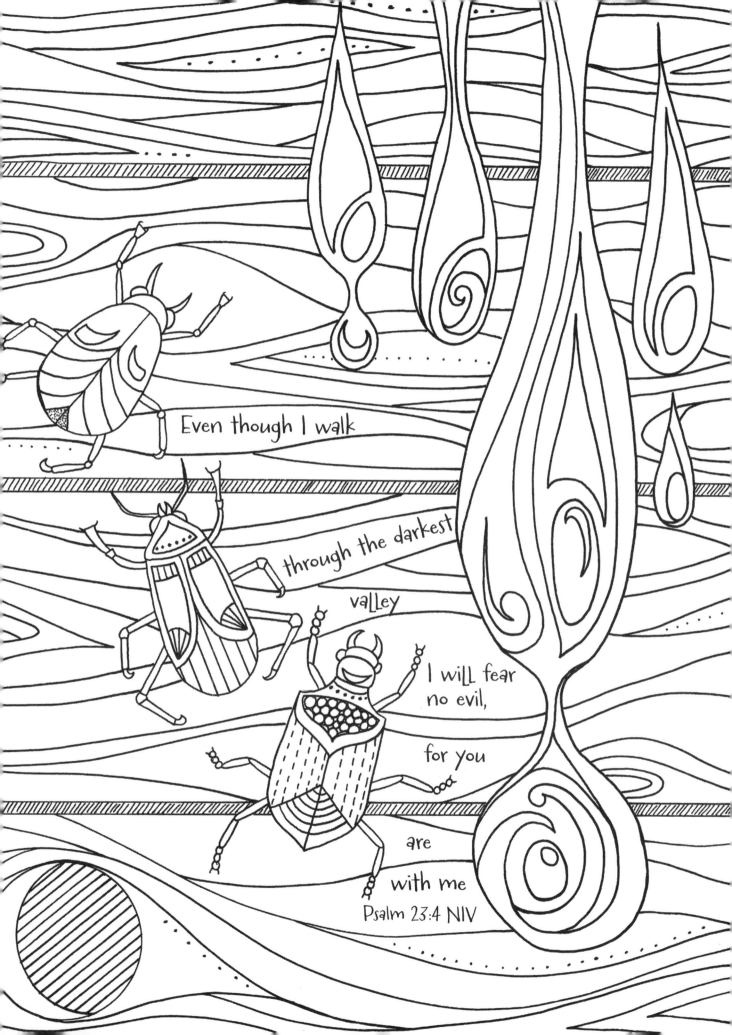

Even though I walk

through the darkest

valley

I will fear
no evil,

for you

are

with me
Psalm 23:4 NIV

Higher than the highest heavens—
that's how high your tender mercy
extends!

Psalm 103:11 TPT

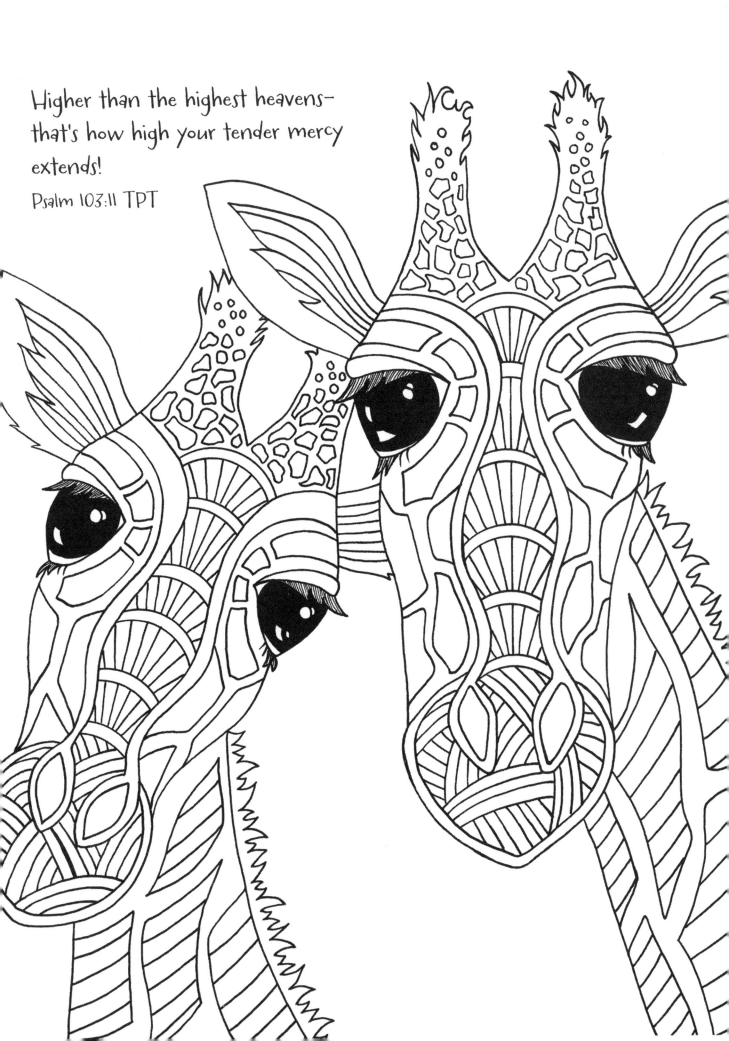

The animals going in were
every living thing, as
Then the Lord

male and female of
God had commanded Noah.
shut him in.

Genesis 7:16 NIV

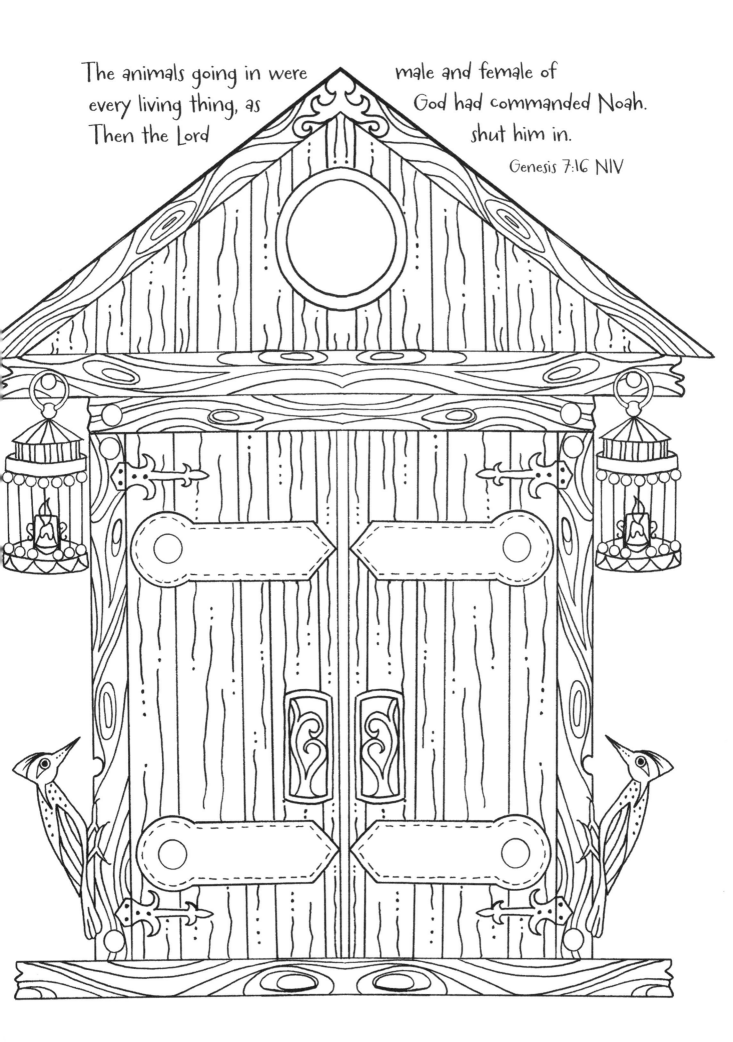

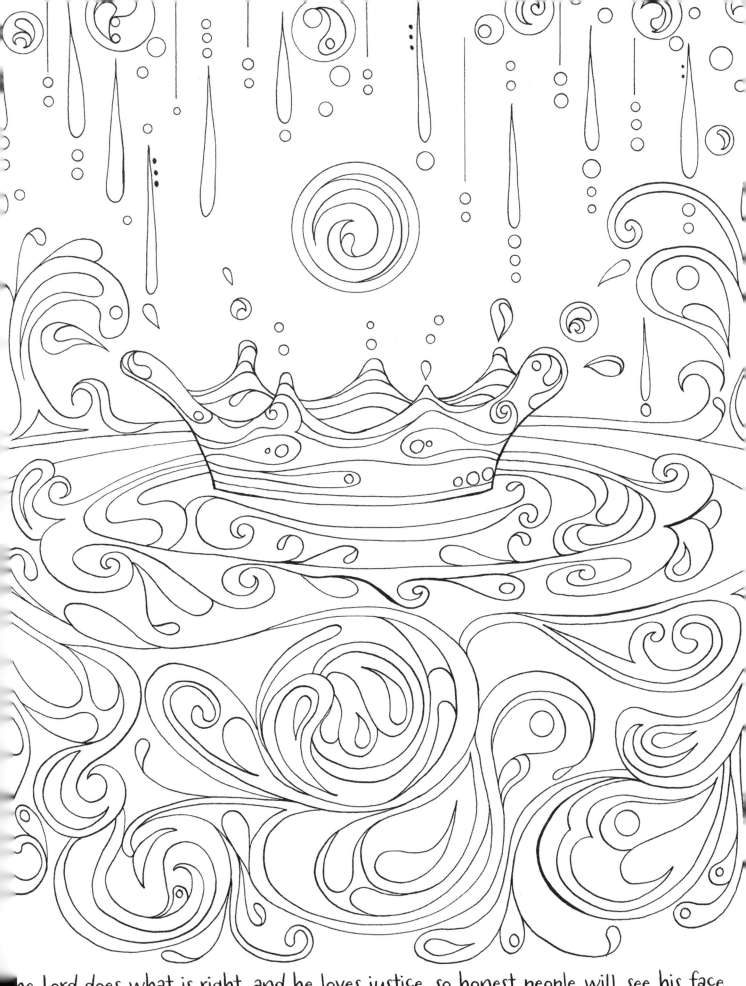

he Lord does what is right, and he loves justice, so honest people will see his face.
Psalm 11:7 NCV

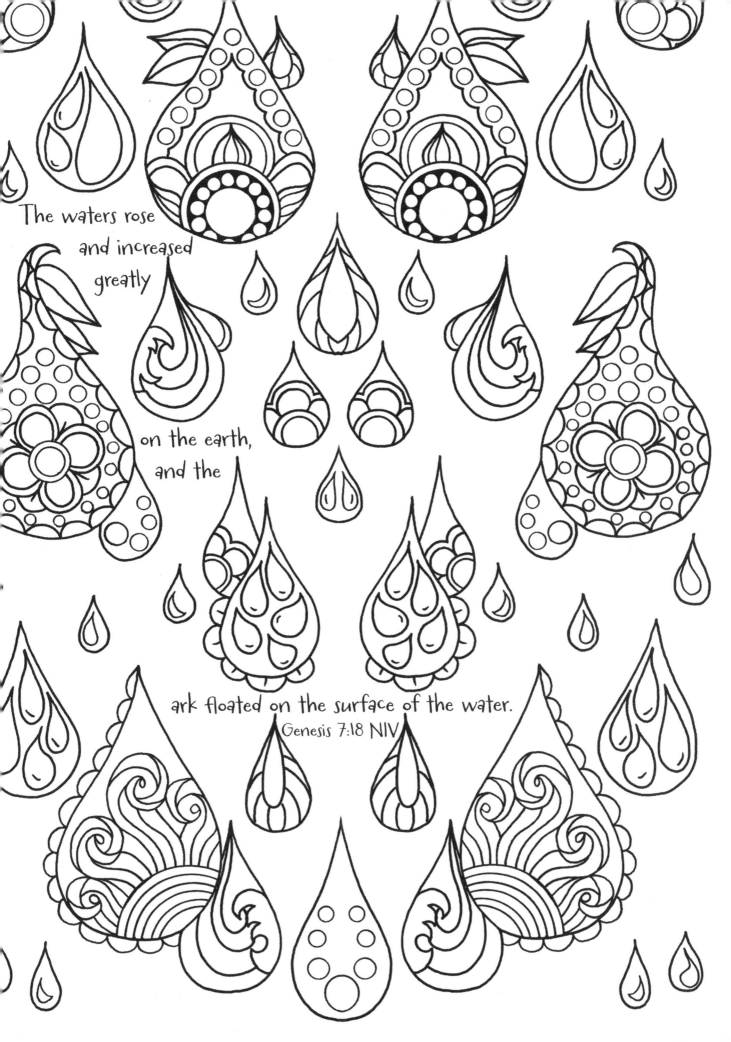

The waters rose and increased greatly on the earth, and the ark floated on the surface of the water.
Genesis 7:18 NIV

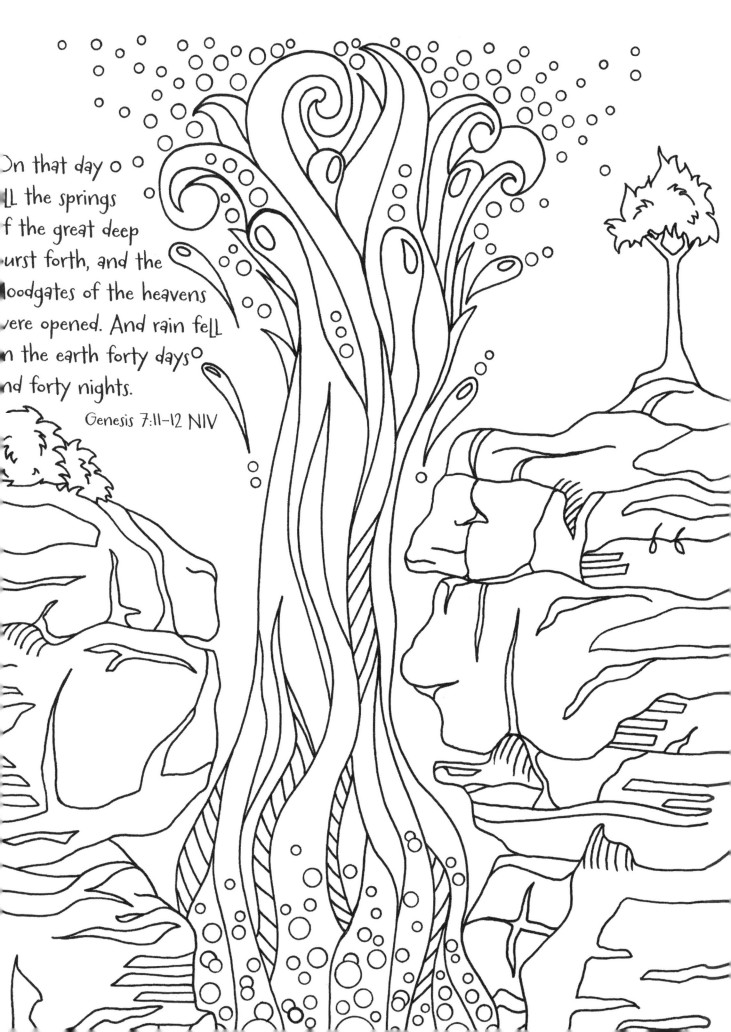

On that day o
ll the springs
f the great deep
urst forth, and the
loodgates of the heavens
ere opened. And rain fell
n the earth forty days
nd forty nights.
Genesis 7:11-12 NIV

The water covered even the highest mountains on the earth, rising more than twenty-two feet above the highest peaks. Genesis 7:19-20 NLT

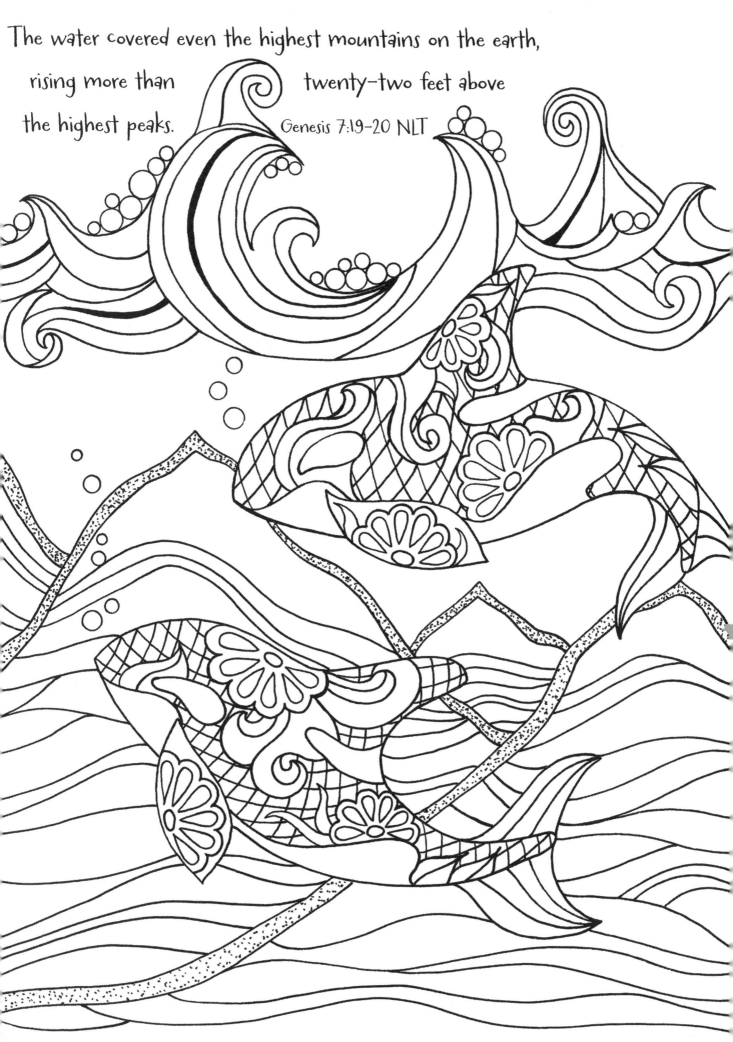

Answer me, O Lord, for your steadfast love is good;
according to your abundant mercy,
turn to me. Psalm 69:16 NRSV

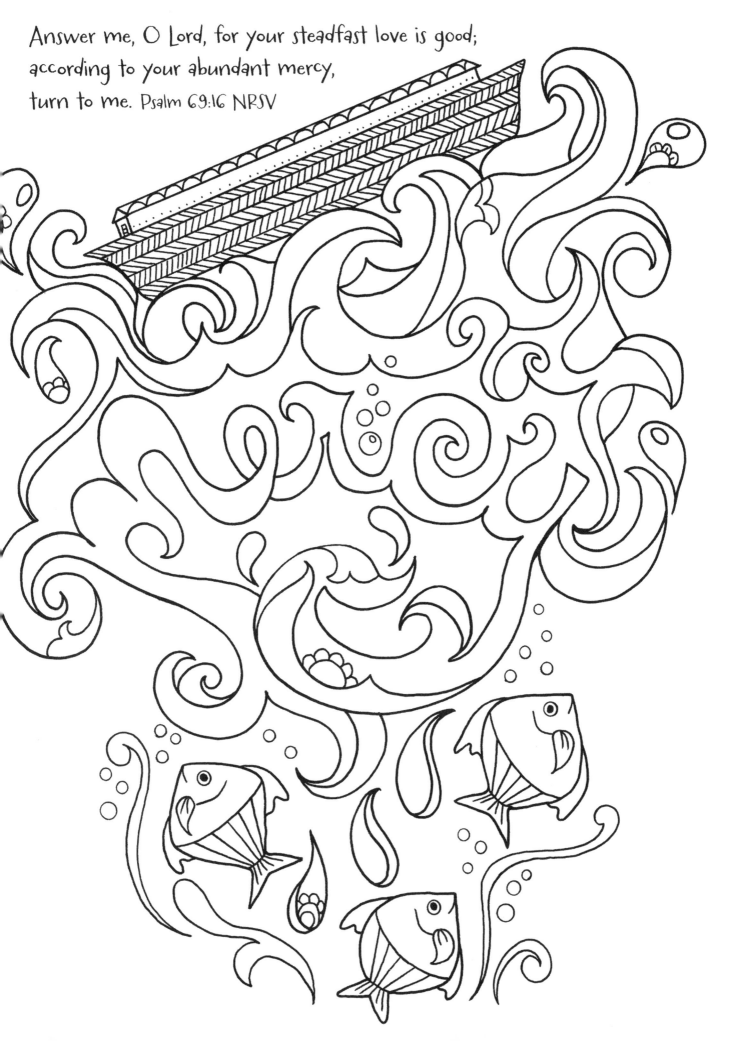

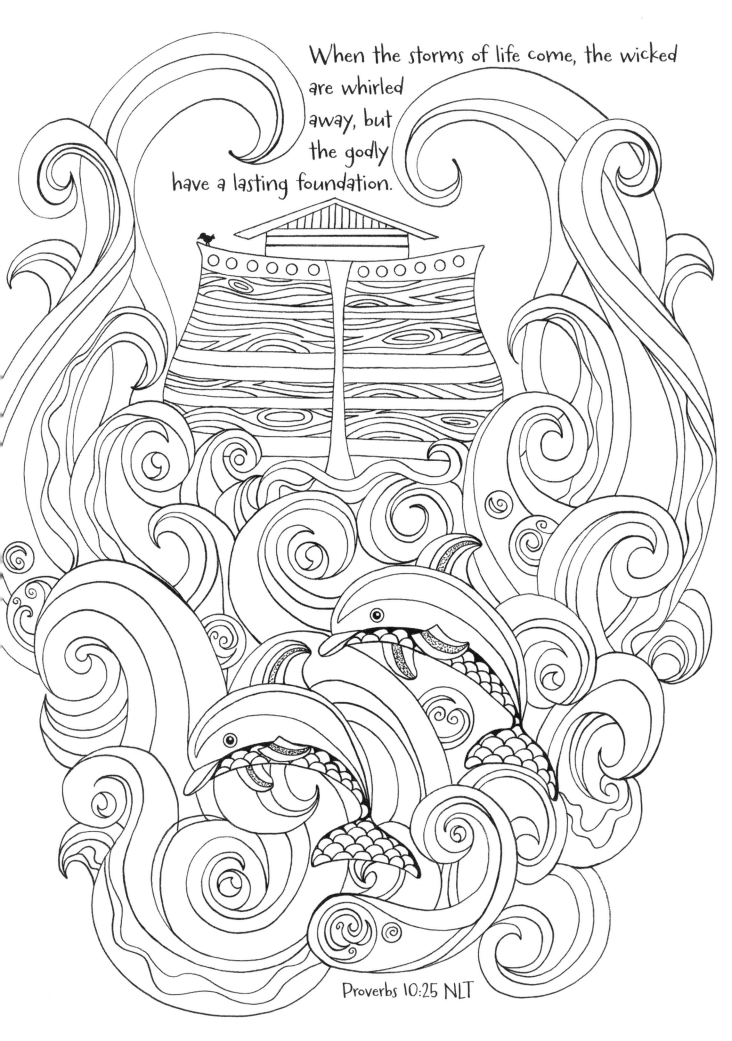

When the storms of life come, the wicked are whirled away, but the godly have a lasting foundation.

Proverbs 10:25 NLT

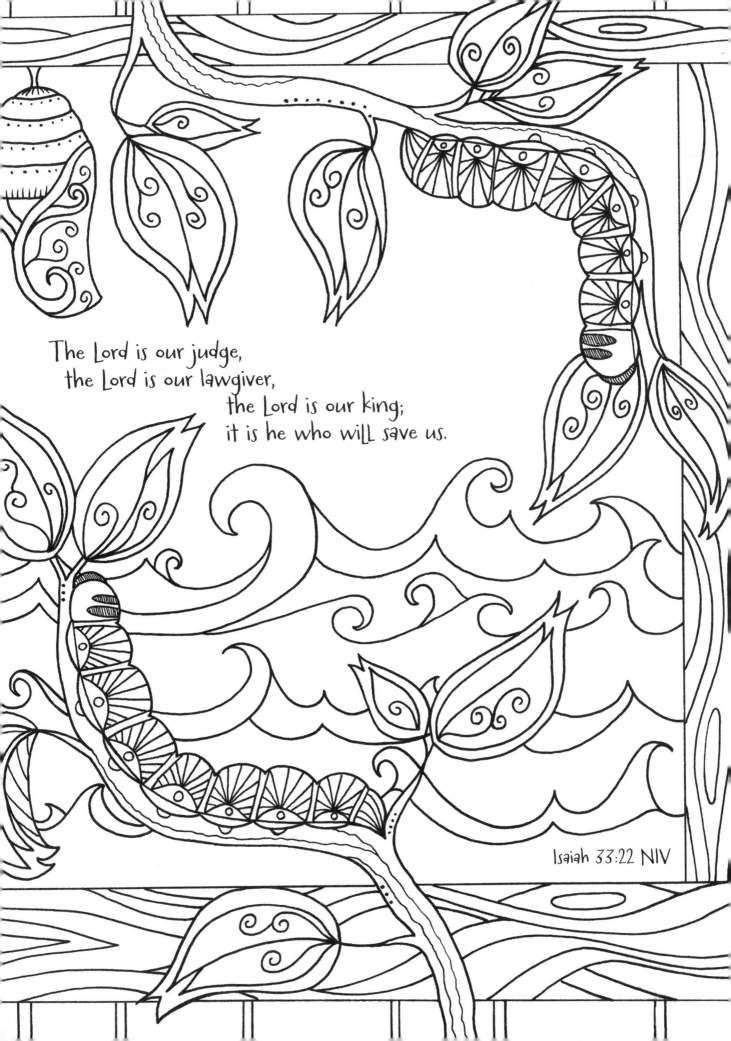

The Lord is our judge,
the Lord is our lawgiver,
the Lord is our king;
it is he who will save us.

Isaiah 33:22 NIV

"I made the light and the darkness. I bring peace, and I cause troubles. I, the Lord, do all these things."

Isaiah 45:7 NCV

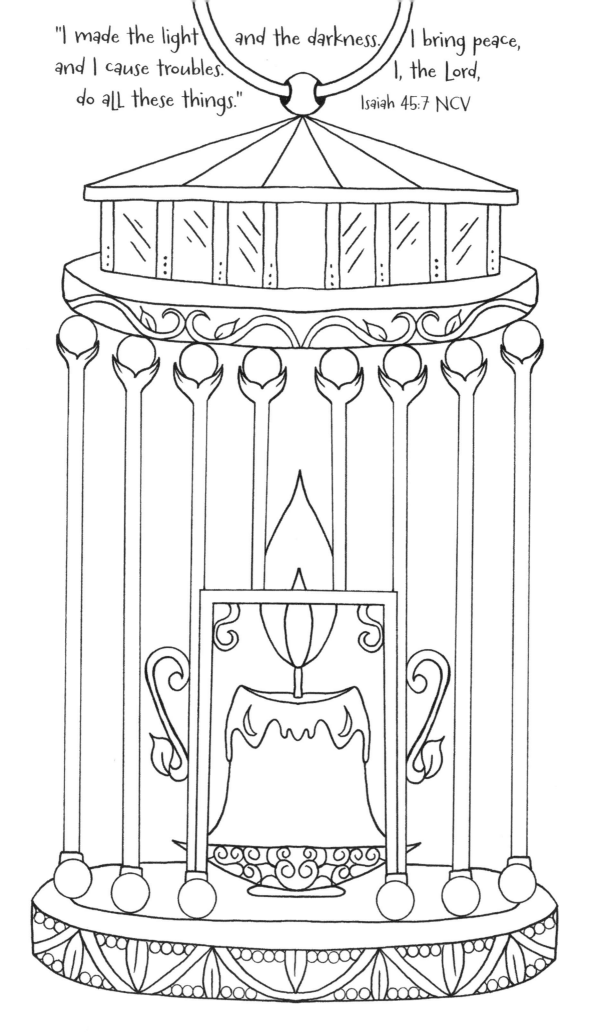

He will bless those who fear the Lord,
Both small and great.

Psalm 115:13 NKJV

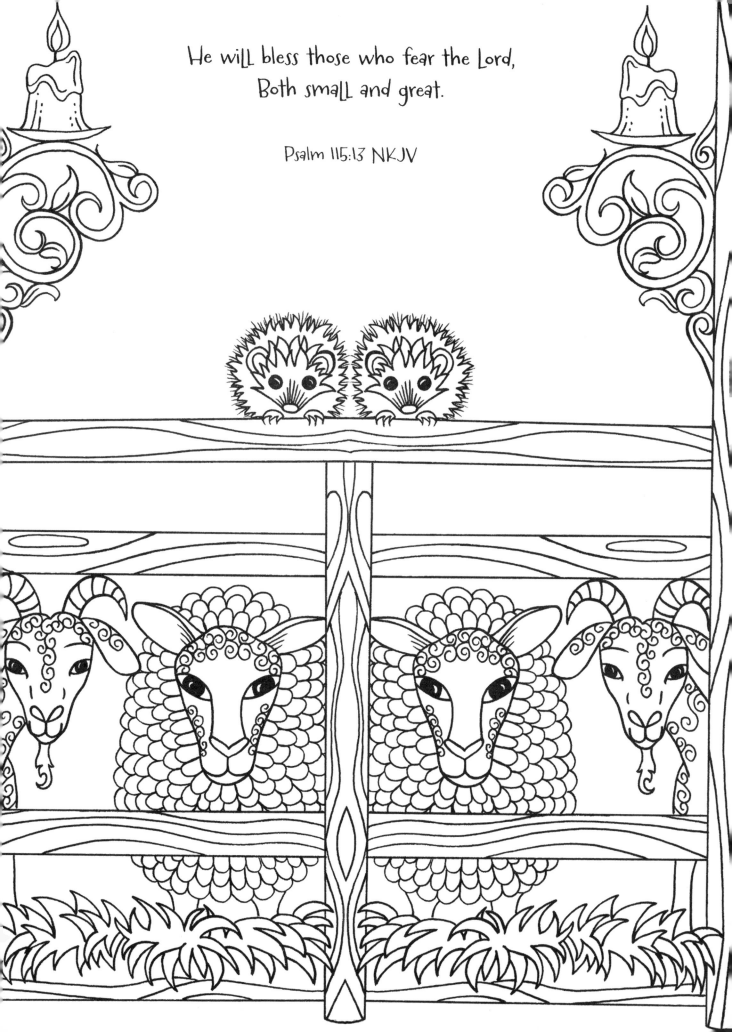

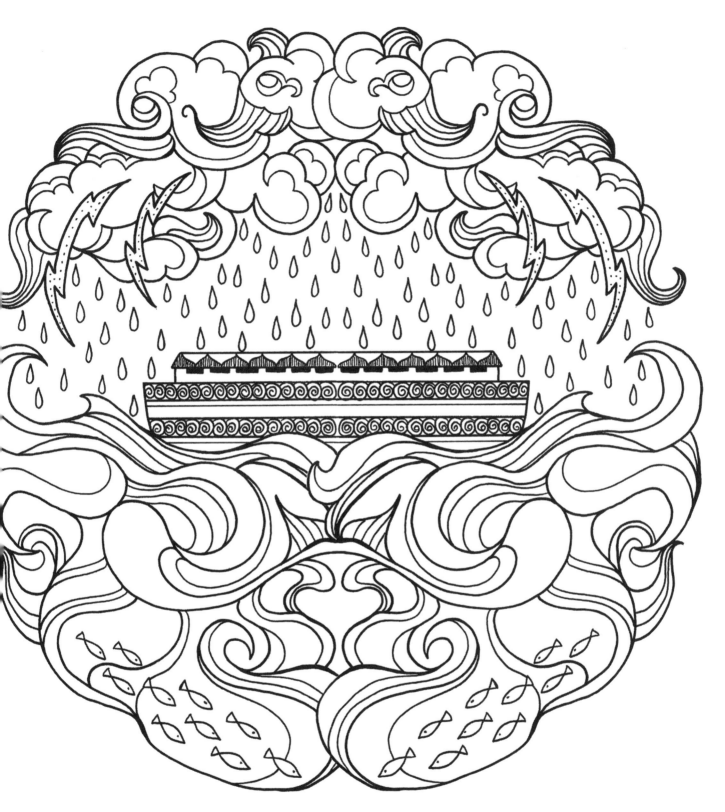

He commanded and raised the stormy wind,
which lifted up the waves of the sea.

Psalm 107:25 NRSV

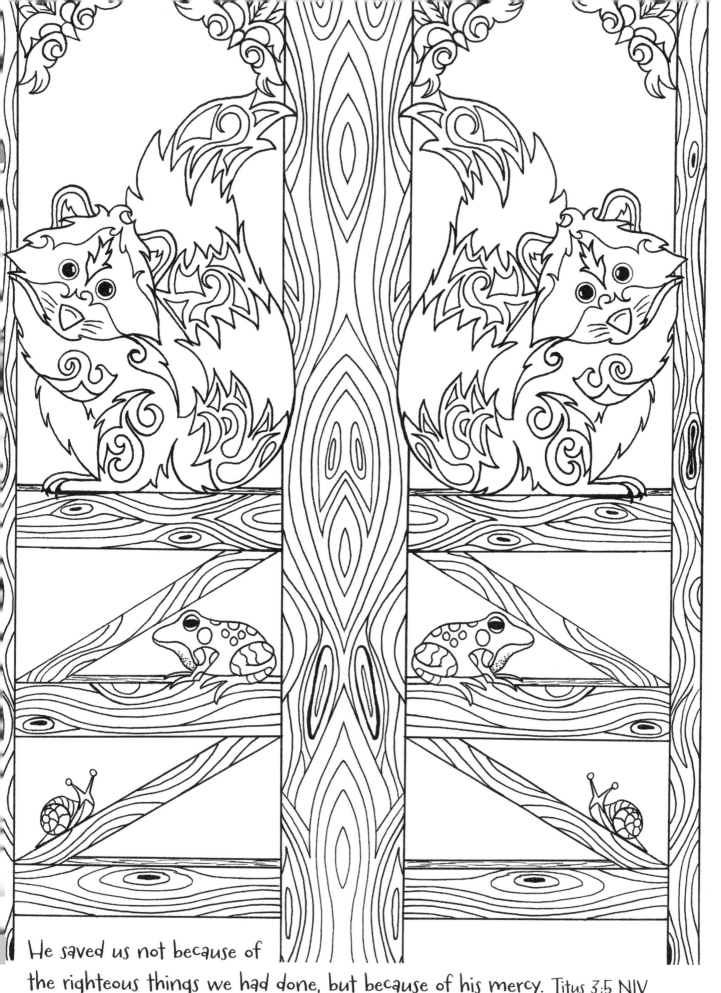

He saved us not because of
the righteous things we had done, but because of his mercy. Titus 3:5 NIV

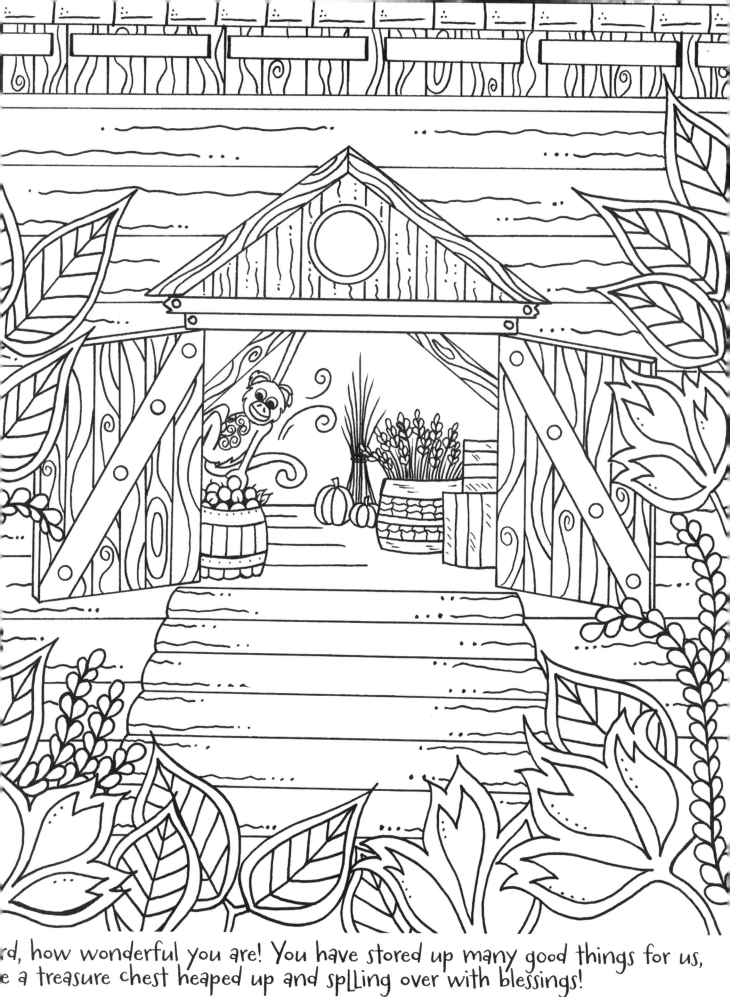

rd, how wonderful you are! You have stored up many good things for us,
e a treasure chest heaped up and spLLing over with blessings!

Psalm 31:19 TPT

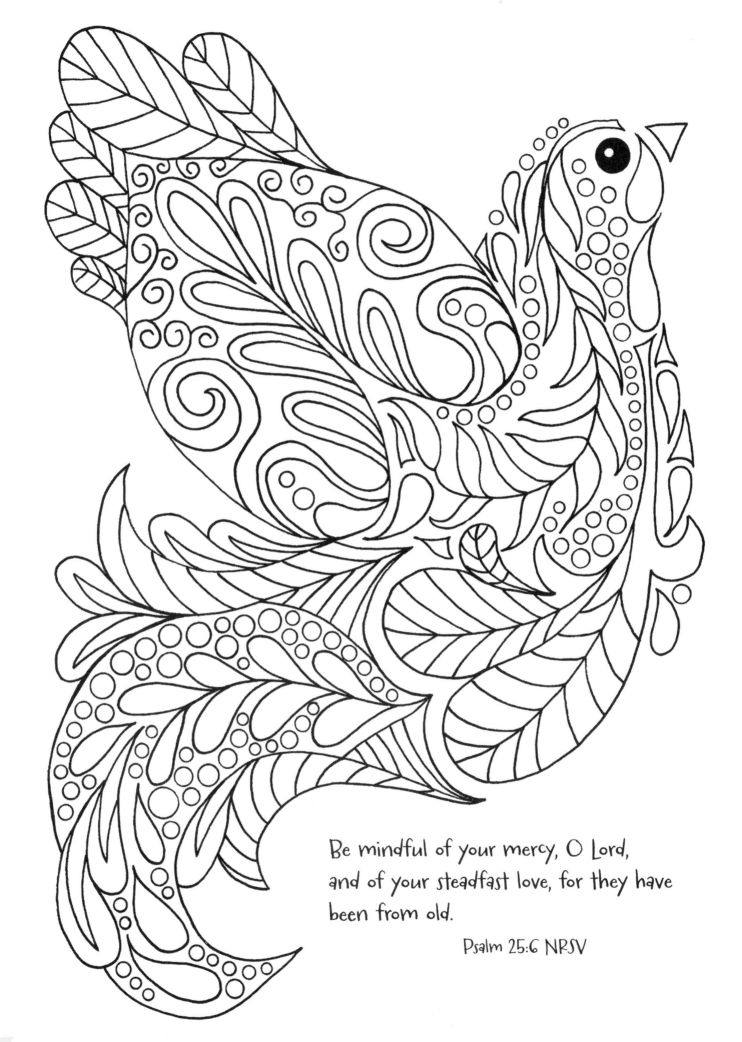

Be mindful of your mercy, O Lord,
and of your steadfast love, for they have
been from old.

Psalm 25:6 NRSV

When the dove returned to him in the evening, there in its beak was a live leaf! Then Noah knew that the water had receded from the earth.

Genesis 8:11 NIV

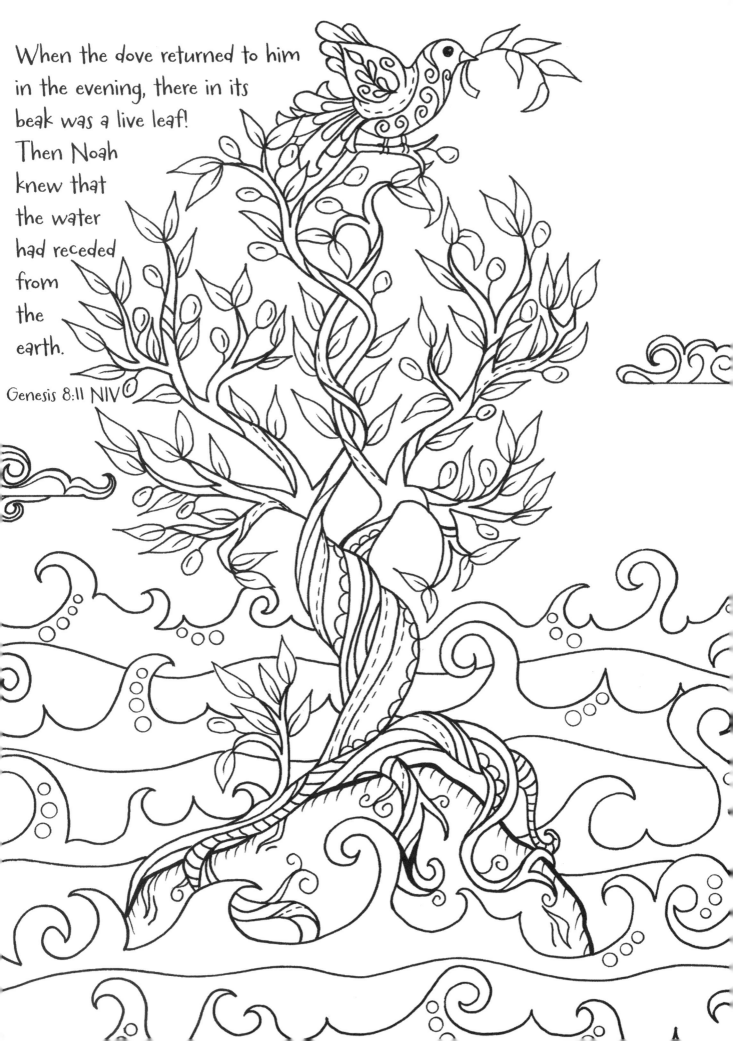

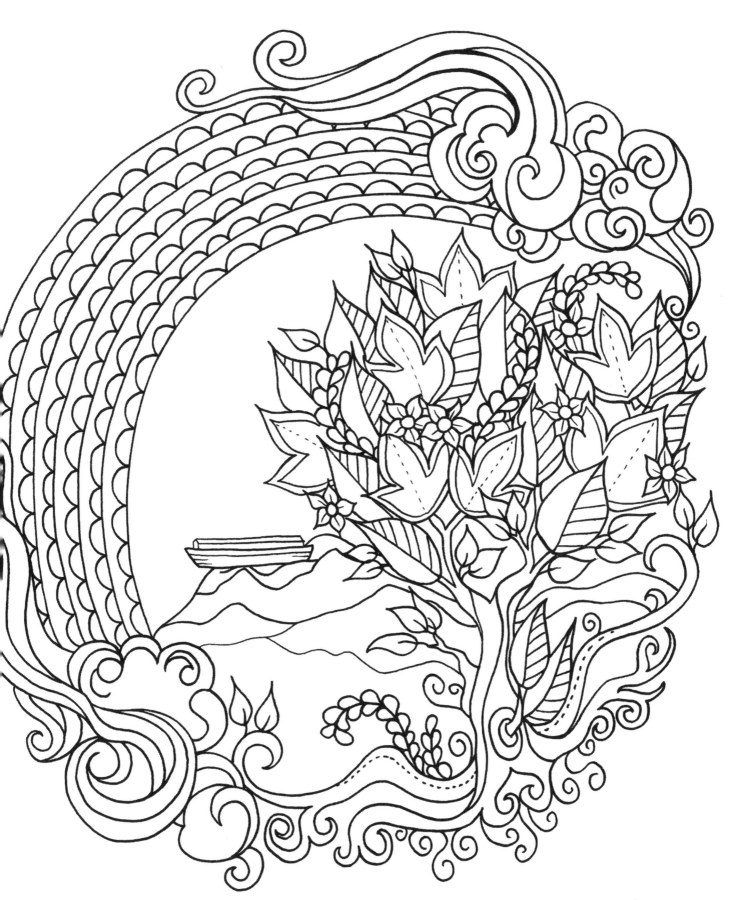

Whenever the rainbow appears in the clouds, I will see it and remember the everlasting covenant between God and all living creatures of every kind on the earth.

Genesis 9:16 NIV

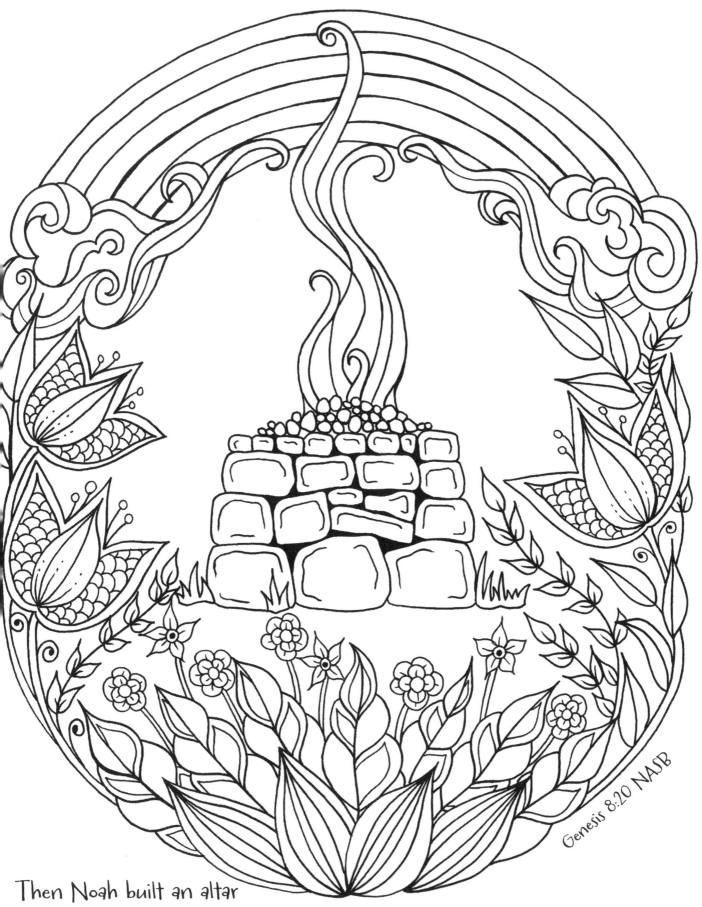

Then Noah built an altar
to the Lord, and took of every clean animal and of every clean bird
and offered burnt offerings on the altar.

Genesis 8:20 NASB

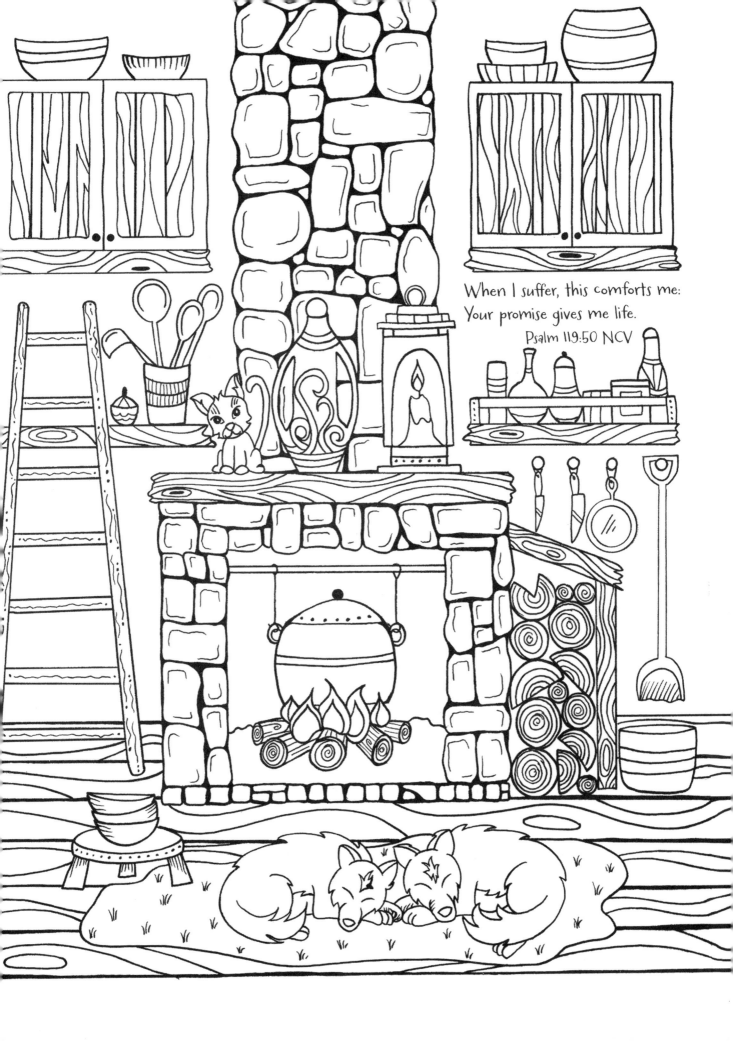

When I suffer, this comforts me:
Your promise gives me life.
Psalm 119:50 NCV

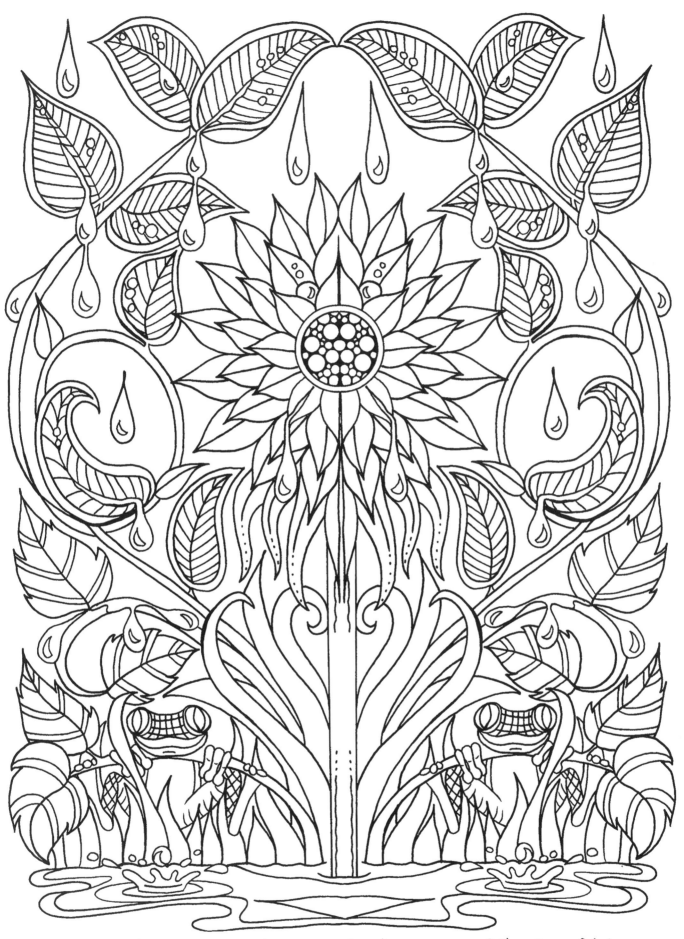

As were the days of Noah, so will be the coming of the Son of Man.
Matthew 24:37 ESV